A Heart-to-Heart Chat on Buddhism

with Old Master Gudo

A Heart-to-Heart Chat on Buddhism

with Old Master Gudo

Gudo Wafu Nishijima

translated by Jundo Cohen

treeleaf
PUBLICATIONS zendo

Cover photograph by Jeremy Pearson

Published by

TREELEAF ZENDO PUBLICATIONS
U.S. Address:
54 Willow Grove Road, Brunswick, Maine 04011 USA
Japan Address:
1331 Numazaki, Tsukuba, Ibaraki, 300-2634 Japan

ISBN: 978-0-692-37433-7

平常心

愚道和夫

BALANCED, ORDINARY MIND
Calligraphy by Gudo Wafu

A Heart-to-Heart Chat on Buddhism
with Old Master Gudo

CONTENTS

A Heart-to-Heart Chat on Buddhism
with Old Master Gudo

TRANSLATOR's FOREWARD

My Teacher, Gudo Wafu Nishijima Roshi, died this year, still sitting daily *Zazen* at age 94. In manner, he was a soft-spoken, gentle, conservative man of his times, born nearly a century ago in Taisho era Japan. In action, he was a perceptive commentator on the current state and future of Zen Buddhism; a critic and outspoken reformer (even if largely ignored by the Buddhist establishment); and a creative and original (if sometimes slightly unorthodox) visionary and philosopher who sought to express Zen and Mahayana Buddhist teachings in unique and helpful ways understandable to people of modern times. I believe that what he stood for will have lasting, positive effects on the future of Soto Zen Buddhism in Japan and the West, and that his many students (not, by any means, all cut of the same cloth) will carry on his legacy. First and foremost, Nishijima cherished *Zazen* as the fulfillment of reality itself, the proper centerpiece of all Buddhist practice.

Nishijima was a traditional Zen teacher in some ways, yet also someone who foresaw great changes in Buddhist customs as practices encounter new times, places and cultures. While he was aware that the outer wrappings of Buddhist traditions may change, he also knew that Buddhist truth transcends time, place and conditions. He was a champion of the celibate way in his own life (Nishijima Roshi, although married and a parent, turned to a celibate lifestyle following his own ordination). Nonetheless, he never felt that celibacy was the way for all, and came to advocate a form of ordination fully stepping beyond and dropping away divisions of priest or lay, male or female. In Nishijima's *Sangha*, we do not ask and are unconcerned with whether we are priest or lay, for we are neither one alone, while always thoroughly both; exclusively each in the purest and unadulterated form, yet wholly all at once. We fully embody and actuate each and all in the moment.

Likewise, Nishijima was a working man all his adult life, and continued so even after ordination right into his final years. In our lineage, the family kitchen, children's nursery, office or factory where we work diligently and hard, the hospital bed, volunteer activity and town hall are all our monastery and place of training. Although Nishijima taught that each of us can benefit from periods of withdrawal and silence, be it in *sesshin* or *ango*, monastic training, or a hermit's hut in the hills, he also knew that Zen priests and Zen training can come in many fruitful forms. For those of us out in the world, priest training can be found right in the city streets, homes, workplaces and soup kitchens of this modern world, as much as behind monastery walls. The barriers of in and out are forgotten; all walls drop away.

Nishijima called for Zen Buddhism in Japan to turn away from the funeral culture that has become the dominant focus of most Buddhist temples in that country, and sought a return to an emphasis on *Zazen*. Nishijima was ordained and received Dharma Transmission from Rempo Niwa Zenji, the Abbot of Eihei-ji, the senior Soto Zen monastery. Knowing that Nishijima was a critic of the very system Niwa Zenji himself headed, Niwa nonetheless empowered Nishijima as a teacher based on Niwa's own shared desire to help reform Soto Zen. (A profile and talk by Niwa Zenji is featured in the Appendix to this book.) Nishijima called for a return to the energy and vibrancy of Buddhist practice which rejects the grayness, rigidity and tangled cobwebs sometimes found in large religious institutions, as most of the major Buddhist sects in Japan have become, and as some large Zen institutions in the West risk becoming.

Nishijima was thoroughly imbued with the spirit of Dogen, was a translator of Dogen's complete *Shobogenzo* into modern Japanese and (with his student Chodo Cross) into English, and felt that Master Dogen had found ways to express the Buddhist teachings rarely heard until the modern day. Nonetheless, despite his profound trust in the teachings of Dogen, I would not describe Nishijima as a prisoner of Dogen. Among the many treasured teachings of Dogen that are timeless and survive the centuries, Nishijima knew that some were primarily the views and expressions of a man living amid the society and superstitions of 13th century Japan, words aimed directly at the needs of monastics pursuing a cloistered life. Those of Dogen's writings directed primarily to his band of monks at Eihei-ji must be placed side by side with Dogen's other pronouncements recognizing the possibilities of Zen practice for people in all situations of life. Buddhism, and Dogen's teachings, can be brought forth and adapted for our situations and times.

Nishijima thought that Zen teachings could best be introduced to a Western audience via finding common ground with Western philosophy, science and modern medicine. Years before it was common to load meditators into MRI machines, Nishijima spoke of the connection of *Zazen* to the brain and human nervous system, influenced by then cutting-edge research on meditation by Harvard's Dr. Herbert Benson and others. Nonetheless, some readers may find that several of Nishijima's ideas and ways of expressing Buddhist teachings were quite personal to him, and his understanding of human physiology as a non-specialist was sometimes a bit simple in description. Even as his student, I wish to say honestly that Nishijima was not a professional philosopher nor a trained scientist. He tried to express from his own heart the sense of balance and clarity encountered in *Zazen*. For that reason, he frequently spoke in very creative but, perhaps, too simplified ways on Western philosophical concepts, and, as a scientific layman, about what happens in the body and brain. Only in recent years have we come to understand that many separate physiological and neurological systems are interlinked in intricate ways, each coming into play in *Zazen*. But regardless of whether or not he was completely accurate in his description of how the body functions in *Zazen*, Nishijima stood for and believed in the meeting and fundamental compatibility of Buddhist tenets and scientific method. Such a belief is a breath of fresh air in the often myth- and superstition-bound world of religions, including Buddhism.

One aspect of Nishijima's teachings that may stand out for some people is his frequent mention of "idealism," "materialism," and the transcending of both via a "realistic" viewpoint and the pure "action" of *Zazen*. In this, Nishijima developed a truly useful and unique way to re-express key perspectives of Mahayana Buddhism and *Shikantaza Zazen*. Nishijima described *Zazen* as a practice of "action" or pure doing/being, and Buddhism as a "realistic" philosophy beyond idealistic religions or materialistic philosophies. He pointed out that most people dream of a world (or in their religious views, of some heaven or enlightenment) that is ideal by our little human standards. They feel a disconnect between how the world appears and how they wish it should be, dreaming of some state much better than the present condition. That, for Nishijima, is an "idealistic" view. Nishijima contrasted such views with those of other people who seem to posit the world as ultimately driven by chance mechanical processes and blind physical forces, going no place in particular, perhaps pointless, meaningless and survival-of-the-fittest cruel. He termed such view "materialism."

However, for Nishijima, Buddhism is an existentialist way of active being in the world *just-as-it-is*. We neither judge the world as lacking in comparison to another ideal world, nor do we judge it as cold, pointless and hopeless. In that way, as Nishijima describes it, a "realistic" view swallows whole both materialism and idealism by finding this world, just going where it goes, to be ideally just what it is; a somehow overridingly positive, beautiful and peaceful sense of the world that fully encompasses this life we find of beautiful or ugly, peace and war, happiness and sadness. Nishijima's words also allow us to encounter the world in seemingly contradictory ways: fully satisfied, at one and at home in this world just-as-it-is while, simultaneously (like Nishijima the social critic himself, holding a vision for societal improvement) able to work to right the wrongs and fix what is broken. Yet, beyond merely relying on words and armchair notions to describe this realistic perspective, we must actually taste and realize to the marrow the practice-experience of *Zazen* and all our life. The balance of body-mind, and the resulting wisdom one encounters, allows us to experience the balance and wholeness, which is this whole world.

Perhaps readers will sometimes feel that Nishijima went a bit far with his model of reality. For example, Nishijima Roshi came to advocate a unique, and very personal, interpretation of the "Four Noble Truths" (contained in this book) as an expression of his views on idealism, materialism and the rest, and some may feel that he stretched things a bit too much. It may be so sometimes. However, the fundamental points he sought to make in doing so—of Zen practice as a way to encounter the sacred in just what is, and *Zazen* as a means to realize the balanced and whole of this world, which often seems so out of balance and broken into pieces—should not be easily discarded. It is an important teaching.

While never completely free of his own idealism and matters of faith, like all of us, perhaps, Nishijima Roshi nonetheless sought to present Zen practice freed of naive beliefs and superstitions, exaggerated claims and idealized myths masquerading as historical events, all of which can bury and hide the very real power of our Buddhist way in a mass of ignorance and foolishness. I, and many of his other students, join him in that task. In such ways, Gudo Wafu Nishijima helped change Zen Buddhism and continues to do so. His legacy lives on in his many students around the world and his teachings will further enrich and transform our tradition into the future.

Finally, I would like to thank Alan Rossi and Kirk McElhearn for their work in helping to edit this text. All remaining errors are due to my sometime failure to follow their good advice. Readers may detect a certain formal, even antiquated manner of expression in my English translation of Nishijima's words. This is the result of my attempt to track closely the writing style and manner of expression of his original Japanese book, and to capture somewhat the elegant way in which Nishijima spoke as a man of his generation and level of reserve and politeness in the Japanese language. I also thank the many other people who have contributed to this publication in countless ways, and to all of Nishijima Roshi's Dharma Heirs around the world. This book will be released for the first anniversary of Nishijima Roshi's passing.

Winter, 2014

Jundo Cohen
Treeleaf Sangha, Tsukuba, Japan

A Heart-to-Heart Chat on Buddhism with Old Master Gudo

INTRODUCTION

What follows in these pages is a friendly conversation over tea between an old Buddhist priest, named "Gudo," and a young student of Buddhism, named "Sekishin," who has many questions about many matters. Of course, you can think of the old priest Gudo as being this writer, while Sekishin is a fictitious composite of the hundreds of students, both Japanese and from numerous other countries of the world, who have come to study with me, and sit *Zazen* with me, over the years. Gudo is the name that was given me so many years ago at the time of my ordination. *Gu* means foolish, and *Do* means truth or way. So, this book represents but the opinions of a foolish old man on the truth. Sekishin means a pure heart, a sincere heart; in other words, the open and sincere heart that a good student should possess.

Buddhism, many people seem to think, is a bewildering philosophy; very dark and dreary, with much talk of suffering. Even in the case of this writer, who has continued in the practice of Buddhism since the time I was an 18-year old schoolboy, through this, my 84th year of life, it sometimes strikes me as nearly impenetrable in aspects; at least at first glance. However, as the cumulative result of these many years of practice, I believe that I have come to some understanding of its fundamental teachings and ways. I also believe that I have come to appreciate several of the reasons Buddhism is perceived as being so very difficult. I wish to provide an explanation of Buddhist concepts in a style that will not be so very hard to understand. This book was written to clearly explain the subtle tenets of Buddhism, yet in an easy-to-understand fashion, conveying the meaning of those tenets to all those interested in beginning or deepening their study of Buddhism.

I intend this book as an expansion of many of the same topics and ideas contained in my earlier book in English, *To Meet the Real Dragon*, but approaching such topics and ideas from different perspectives, offering deeper explanation on various important points that I only touched upon briefly in the earlier book. As I think you will understand as you read on, when one seeks to address issues regarding religious philosophy in the form of a question and answer dialogue, many important issues will pop up unexpectedly, and the conversation will wander off in various directions. I knew, in the back of my mind while planning this book, that this was bound to happen. Still, I believe that our dialogue never wanders too far off the track.

Also, issues of religion, by their very nature, are closely linked to the particular personality and deeply-held perspectives of each respective seeker and believer who inquires into them. They are subjects that go right to the heart of matters of life and death, to the very meaning of our being. To attempt to answer such important and delicate questions with a simple yes or no requires great restraint and discretion. But, as I look back, I feel that one reason that Buddhism has been perceived as difficult to understand and abstract in meaning is that, in religious discussions about it, no ultimate conclusions are ever reached due to a spirit of accommodation, elasticity and hesitancy to take hard positions in dealing with the issues addressed. The conclusion is often that position A is right, but position B is right too; and then again, they are both wrong! Other questions are simply avoided. Such a fluid, multi-layered vision is central to the perspectives of Zen, and is a statement of truth in all its diversity. I do not mean to imply otherwise, nor to abandon the wisdom of seeing reality from all angles, as well as from no angle at all. However, in writing this book, I have sought to explore various subjects and issues that Buddhist writers have generally avoided, and I have tried as best I can to offer clear conclusions. Accordingly, should the results of my having done so give rise to some discourtesy or discomfort to those who may hold other points of view, please know that I mean this book merely as one stepping stone in efforts to reform and rebuild a Buddhism for the future which is more correctly viewed and understood for its true meaning; as a Buddhism grounded in *Zazen*, a reform of return to that which *never, ever* can be left. I ask your indulgence in that effort.

I offer *Gassho* to Jundo Cohen, my student and Dharma Heir, for the great care taken by him in his translation from Japanese and reshaping of this book, originally published as *Gudo Rojin Bukkyo Mondo*.

Gudo Wafu Nishijima

木之葉禪堂

港道　知大提香

KO NO HA (Treeleaf) ZENDO
Calligraphy by Gudo Wafu

I. BEGINNINGS

A CUP OF TEA...

Gudo: So very good to see you, Sekishin. Do sit down, relax, have a cup of tea.

Sekishin: I am so sorry to disturb you, Roshi, as you are very busy.

Gudo: No need to say such things. There's nothing better than having a chance to talk about Zen and all of Buddhism. Let's take our time and have a nice heart-to-heart chat. And as there's not enough time just today, let's get together to continue our chat when you come again; as often as you wish.

Sekishin: I would like that very much.

IS RELIGION TRULY NECESSARY?

Sekishin: Well, Roshi, the first thing I would like to ask is whether something like religion is truly necessary in society, or in our personal lives. One sees that there are people all around who believe in some religion or other. But, these days, one also sees so many people who claim not to belong to any formal religion. Of course, when there is some unhappiness close to home, or at special times in life such as a wedding or funeral, most people will turn to some religion, be it Buddhism, Christianity or whatever appeals to the person or family. Still, that doesn't mean that those people, or all of those family members, really have faith in that religion. I know many people who claim proudly that they don't believe in any religion, yet it doesn't seem to me that such people are thereby necessarily less happy in their lives. A great number do as well as so-called "religious" people in leading happy, healthy and successful lives, and there are many examples of friends with sound and happy home lives not grounded in any religion. On the other hand, when I look at how people are doing who have deep religious belief, I find that, well, that does not spare them or their family members from falling sick, or suffering at the hands of economic circumstances or other hardships, or from meeting all kinds of terrible tragedies. So, I would like to ask just what function religion serves.

Gudo: Ah, it is very good to think about whether religion is necessary or not. There are so many people who simply believe in some religion blindly without questioning, and others who dismiss all religions as foolish out of hand, all without really examining this very important question. Truly, I believe that all human beings, almost *without exception*, have a religion, that all men and women are religious, even those who think that they are not religious and describe themselves as agnostic, atheistic, anti-religious or such.

Sekishin: Why do you think that, Roshi?

Gudo: Well, if I am going to answer that question, there is another question that needs to be addressed first.

Sekishin: And that is?

Gudo: That is the question of what religion is in the first place.

Sekishin: I see. So, if we don't think first about what religion really is, we can't begin to address the question of whether religion is necessary after all.

Gudo: That is right.

RELIGION IN COMMON UNDERSTANDING

Sekishin: Alright. So, what is religion?

Gudo: Before I give you my own definition of religion, and explain why almost all men and women necessarily possess one, I first would like to look at the definition and characteristics of a religion in common, popular understanding; religion as ordinarily viewed. To address that, we must look at the various types of religion that exist, and try roughly to categorize each of them.

Sekishin: Yes. There are so many in the world. Buddhism, Christianity, Judaism, Islam, Hinduism, Taoism, Confucianism, and on and on.

Gudo: Well, those are enough for us to focus on for the moment. What happens if we look for some common point or characteristic that runs through each of those religions?

Sekishin: That seems pretty hard to do. However, I suppose that if we were to speak of a common characteristic, almost every religion has some idea of a God or a Buddha, an entity existing above us, and that such entity constitutes the absolute in some way.

Gudo: Yes. That is without question one of the characteristics shared by each of what are commonly thought of these days as a religion. Is there anything else?

Sekishin: Well, in addition, I think that there is a tendency in most religions to downplay the physical or material aspect of our being, and to place much greater importance upon some spiritual element. For example, if we look at tales such as the story of Adam and Eve in the Old Testament, we are given the feeling that there is some impure or sinful aspect to the physical realm, such as in the physical relationship of man and woman, and that somehow we should seek a way to free ourselves from that bondage. We are told that there is something higher and purer, standing in contrast to the low and unclean face of earthly existence.

Gudo: Yes, I believe that to be a common characteristic of religions as conceived by most people as well.

Sekishin: Moreover, as the flip side of a relative contempt for matters of the flesh, for the primarily material, religions have a tendency to raise up the spiritual, to praise matters of the soul, such as by belief in some spiritual essence or existence beyond the human.

Gudo: That is right too. Anything more?

Sekishin: Well, I think I have reached the end of my ideas.

Gudo: You have pointed out several characteristics that are common to most religions. First, they view as absolute some entity transcending the human world. Second, they revere the spiritual and tend to scorn matters of the physical and material. Third, they believe in some spiritual essence or existence beyond our human form, such as a soul. I think all of those are the characteristics of religion in common understanding. They are closely intertwined, and if I were to further add something related to all this, it would be a denial or dissatisfaction with the present world, and a longing for some world-to-come. Anyway, those are the characteristics of a religion in common understanding. However, my definition of a religion is a bit different and is something that virtually no human being can avoid having.

RELIGION IN COMMON UNDERSTANDING & BUDDHISM

Sekishin: Roshi, you have referred several times here to religion as viewed in common understanding, but mentioned that your view of the definition of religion is a bit different. What do you mean by that?

Gudo: Well, speaking honestly, I doubt whether something should be thought of as a religion only if it bears the previously mentioned characteristics, or only because it is thought of as a religion in common opinion.

Sekishin: What exactly do you mean by that?

Gudo: To simplify, after comparing what you have pointed out just now as the common characteristics of religion, and contrasting those to something that I have examined and thought about deeply over many, many years—namely, the characteristics of Buddhism—I have found some very interesting differences that exist in the case of Buddhism.

STATUE OF GAUTAMA BUDDHA IN *ZAZEN*

If we look at the first characteristic of religion, namely, belief in an entity transcending the human world, and if we seek out the characteristics of Buddhism, I doubt whether Buddhism has such a characteristic. Of course, in Buddhism there is a Buddha. It appears on first impression that in Buddhism, a "Buddha" corresponds more or less to the idea of a god as known in other religions. However, the founder of Buddhism, Gautama Buddha, was clearly but a human being, not a god. Gautama Buddha was born some two and a half millennia ago in the Lumbini Garden near the city of Kapilvastu, in a part of northeastern India which is now in Nepal. It is said that he was born as the prince of a small kingdom, yet at the age of 29 he left home, at the age of 35 he achieved the truth that he would then spread in his wanderings across the land, and at the age of 80 he died at Kushinagar. Accordingly, Gautama Buddha's life, if we look at it honestly, was just the life of an ordinary human being.

HIGHLY IDEALIZED IMAGE OF "BUDDHA DESENDING FROM HEAVEN"

8

Of course, after his death, certain Buddhist followers sought to exalt the man and his teachings by portraying him as superhuman, by depicting him in statues of gold and the like. They created idealized legends and miraculous images, attributing to him all manner of magical powers and fabulous perfections. But such a view of Buddha, who was a man, is to be found nowhere in the true message of Buddhism.

Sekishin: So, are you saying that Buddha is just the name of a human being?

Gudo: Exactly. In Chinese Buddhism, for example—in the teachings of the famous Zen Master Rinzai and others—expressions such as *The True Man of No Rank* are sometimes used. This expresses that there is much to the Buddha, and all of us, beyond what the eye can easily see and appraise. But the meaning of this and similar phrases is also that the Buddha was a true human being, nothing more.

The second characteristic that was raised as common to most religions, namely, that generally there is a focus on the spiritual and a disdain for this material world, also stands in marked contrast to Buddhism. From the very beginning of Buddhism, as an expression of the basic standpoint of Buddhist philosophy, phrases such as *The Oneness of Body and Mind* and *The Oneness of Mind and Phenomena* have been used. These represent a perspective that the mind and the physical body are one, cannot be separated, and that the physical and any spiritual, sacred aspect of this universe are but two faces of a single whole. This is the identity of *Samsara*, this ordinary world, and *Nirvana*. The physical and the spiritual shall never be apart, and this very world in which we live is sacred, just as it is. Everything in this world, be it the magnificent mountain, be it the rotting trash heap; all are sacred. Moreover, the idea of The Oneness of Body and Mind and of The Oneness of Mind and Phenomena are absolutely necessary for a proper understanding of Buddhism. Thereby, in the Buddhist view at least, it is not possible to defend an attitude holding high only that which is of the spirit, denigrating that which is of the physical, material world, for all is one.

Sekishin: And what about the third characteristic?

Gudo: Ah. The third characteristic is the existence of some soul or spirit. When I was a child, I used to think of Buddhism as a religion that believes in the existence of a soul, in reincarnation and the like, and thus we do such things as perform funeral and memorial services, or offer the reading of *sutras* for the spirits of the dead. However, I was later very surprised to find that Master Dogen, in his *Bendowa*, denied the concept of the imperishability of a soul, stating: *"It is but an heretical view that the spirit, when the body deteriorates, is released here and is born anew elsewhere, that though it seems to die here, it is born there, that it never dies and continues eternally. This is an heretical view."* By this, Dogen stated clearly that the idea of a spirit freed from the body after death and born into some other world—that it is but the spirit that continues on in life after the body's demise—is a teaching of Brahmanism, which was prevalent prior to the advent of Buddhism, but is not a teaching of Buddhism. Yes, the Buddha, as a man of his times and culture, may have taught some vision of rebirth even without a soul. That is true. But even if so, our way does not focus on what may or may not occur after death, a question whose answer we cannot know for sure. Thus, our focus is on just living the life before us, being a complete human being here and now.

Sekishin: This is the first time that I've heard explained that Buddhism does not believe in the immortality of a soul or like ideas, and that rebirth need not be central to Buddhist practice. I am really surprised, and now I am a bit confused as to how best to think about Buddhism.

Gudo: I think that your surprise is reasonable. Even I recall that I received quite a shock the first time I read that passage from the *Bendowa*. But reading those words truly stimulated my young mind and caused me to want to set off on a study of Buddhism and a study of the *Shobogenzo*. So, you never know what is going to change you life.

Sekishin: And what about the fourth characteristic?

Gudo: Well, we can say the same thing about the fourth characteristic we mentioned, a denial of this present world and a longing for some world to come. Some 2,400 years ago, when Gautama Buddha attained the truth under the bodhi tree at Bodhgaya, that which he experienced as reality was expressed thus in the sutras: *"Myself, as well as this earth which bears upon it myself, as well as each and all of the creatures alive which inhabit this earth, are already but truth."* These words are understood to be a testimonial to the very moment of achieving awareness. Even if we look just at this one example, we see that the philosophy of Buddhism is, at its very basis, not a denial or rejection of this world of ours, but a recognition of this very world, and all that is in it, as already enlightenment itself. In looking at these words, it is not easy to think that there is some hidden longing for a world to come.

Sekishin: So, Roshi, does that mean that we can look upon Buddhism as not possessing any of the four characteristics that people think of as usually shared in common by religions?

Gudo: That is right. Up to this point in time, I have not found many other commentators who discuss Buddhism from the point of view I am expressing here, but if we study Buddhism via Master Dogen's *Shobogenzo* and other works, and if we truly taste Buddhism through our *Zazen* meditation morning and night, we find that the religion called Buddhism can be thought of as different from what most people usually think of as a religion.

Sekishin: Thus, are you saying that Buddhism is not a religion?

Gudo: No, that is not necessarily so. But it does lead us to the next stage, which is to address the very serious question of just what, after all, is a religion.

WHAT IS A RELIGION?

Sekishin: So, Roshi, you have said that you have your own, rather different definition of a religion. What do you think of as being a religion?

Gudo: Well, that is terribly difficult, yet an extremely important problem, and we could fill hours and hours talking about it. However, since we could go on and on discussing this before arriving at any conclusion, I will just move directly to stating my own conclusion. For me, there are two elements central to a religion. The first is that there is a way of thinking or ideology believed true concerning the meaning and workings of the world and humankind's place in it. The second is that there is a goal of regulating the actions of the individual to be in accordance with that way of thinking. One aspect

11

of that which constitutes a religion is a faith in some ideology that is a world-view, and the other aspect is a discipline and regulation of the faithful's actions to accord with the ideology thought proper in that faith. It is by this definition that I believe that all men and women, almost without exception, have a religion.

Sekishin: But isn't it true that no such description would apply with regard to, for example, the religions of so-called primitive peoples, such as those of ancient Africa or certain Pacific islands?

Gudo: We can clearly find the two elements present even in the case of any so-called primitive religions. For example, imagine the case of a native tribe that worships the mountain located near their territory, fearing a powerful god thought to reside on that mountain. In such case, they would believe in an ideology regarding their world and their place in it, namely, that the god who lives on the mountain possesses absolute strength, and is controlling some or all aspects of their lives. The act of making food offerings to the god of the mountain, or of performing ritual dances or similar ceremonies, can be seen as expressions, through personal action, of their faith in that way of thinking.

Sekishin: So are you saying that, likewise, in the cases of Christianity and Buddhism and such other religions practiced today in so-called developed societies, one center point of the content of each is their particular ideology concerning the true nature of the world and humankind's place in the world, the way of thinking they respectively possess and which is then acted upon by the upholders of the ideology in their lives?

Gudo: That is correct. The basis for answering the question of what constitutes any religion is by looking at the way of thinking that a religion upholds in its faith.

A THEORY OF EVOLUTION IN RELIGION

Sekishin: Which means that, in accordance with what they each uphold as their thinking, there really are almost countless numbers of what could be termed "religions".

Gudo: That is correct. However, if we compare religions, we find that in the long course of history, and just as occurs among living things in nature when the theory of evolution is seen at work, those religions having some strong or superior quality in their aspect have tended to survive, while those inferior in aspect have tended to disappear. I feel it is so if we examine history.

Sekishin: Are you saying that each of the religions now existing, active and thriving in various ways is, thereby, a strong or superior religion in some way?

Gudo: Yes. I think that one would not be wrong to think in such manner.

Sekishin: Conversely, is it the case that, in the future as well, there will continue to be a survival of the fittest competition among religions, and that even among those religions that are currently popular and widespread, there are some religions that must decay and decline in accordance with the process?

Gudo: Yes, because religions must follow the demands of the inevitable forces of change, just as all phenomena, and it is not possible to say that religions are the sole exception to the process.

THREE TYPES OF RELIGION

Sekishin: Might I ask you now to tell me what you think about various specific religions that are currently widely active and popular. What are their respective good points and bad points?

Gudo: Well, to speak about those respective religions properly it would be necessary to demonstrate plentiful knowledge and experience with each one. As you know, I am a Buddhist priest and, therefore, I may rightly claim to have some knowledge about Buddhism. But I can only speak as an outsider with regard to other religions. Thus, if someone who is an outsider, as I am, were to self-righteously assert his opinions regarding some other religion, I believe that would be very insulting to the followers of

13

the other religion, and further, would run the great risk of making mistakes and misstatements. Therefore, I do not wish to speak about such things.

Instead of doing what you asked, I would like to briefly discuss my general, abstract ideas regarding the three types of religion which exist.

Sekishin: What do you mean by *the three types of religion*?

Gudo: By this, I mean that, if we attempt to classify the religions found in this world in which we live based upon their content, they can be divided into three broad types.

Sekishin: Please tell me about each of these types.

Gudo: The three types consist of those religions that set high store on the ideal, those that venerate the material, and those that emphasize action. By the latter term, I mean a religion that simply tells us to live, to act here and now, in this world *just as it is*. Thus, I call this last kind a religion of "action". Buddhism, I believe, falls within this last category.

Sekishin: I think that this is the first time that I have heard such a classification …

Gudo: Well, perhaps it contains within it my own particular view of religion. However, I believe it is a useful description. A few minutes ago, I expressed my idea that, if we consider religion as commonly understood and Buddhism, they are really quite different in their content with regard to the four characteristics that define a religion, and the categories of religion that I want to describe are derived from that fact.

Sekishin: To begin, the first type, those religions that set high value on the *ideal*, what kind of religion are they?

Gudo: Those are what we usually think of as religions in common understanding. For example, in most religions, the central focus of the teaching is the idea of a superhuman, ideal entity such as a god, and each such religion is formed having as its centerpiece a belief in that god. This type of religion is most like what we usually bring to consider as being a religion, and thus is the most conventional. If we ask the true nature of the entity represented by these idealized, yet anthropomorphic, human-like gods, we can say that it is actually a concept of the ideal which we human beings each carry within our hearts.

We human beings are the animal that has developed the highest ability to think. Accordingly, each moment of each day, we think that we wish circumstances to be like *this*, or to be like *that*, or that things *should be* like this or *should be* like that. We contrast this with the state of the world before us, the state of circumstances we see around us, that are just as they are with all their seeming imperfections. In such manner, the state of the way that things *should be* that we human beings have the capability to envision within our heads is typically called the ideal. Those religions that arose centered upon such higher ideals, focused on images of the ideal, and setting high value on the ideal, are the ones we most usually think of as being religions. Christianity, Judaism, Hinduism, Islam, and many others—even many flavors of Buddhism—most belief systems that we commonly call religions belong to this category. They each hold up some perfect, idealized state or other world, in the light of which this world we live in is just a shadow. They point to some other state of being, or some heaven, toward which we aim, but in contrast to which human beings and the unsightly human world fall far, far short.

Sekishin: And what type of religions worship the *material*?

Gudo: Those are religions that we usually do not think of as, or call, religions. Religions that place importance on the ideal have been very successful; many people belong to such religions, and regulate their lives in accordance with the beliefs and tenets thereof. As a result, a skeptical portion of such believers have come to feel certain contradictions and dissatisfactions in their religion and faith, leading them to doubt the dogma of the religion. The reason is that the ideals commonly upheld by the religion, and the explanations it gives for why the world functions in the way it does, seem to diverge from the actual realities of the world in which we live and are not always in accord with our understanding of how the world really functions. Their assertions frequently appear as farfetched superstitions. Where the two disagree with each other, or point in very different directions, people will suffer the dilemma of whether they should carry through with the asserted ideal or act in the manner that experienced reality seems to indicate. They will be greatly frustrated by how our day-to-day world seems constantly to fall short of the religious ideal, and by how the explanations of the idealized religion seem to offer only fanciful stories to explain the way the world is, unlikely stories that require a good deal of faith and suspension of reason to be believed.

Thereby, from such experience, people will start to doubt the ideals that their religion seems to uphold, which may lead them to criticize those ideals, and which may then lead such people to begin to separate themselves or rebel from the religion, perhaps ultimately following beliefs and tenets that are fully the opposite of what the religion upheld. Such a position is commonly called *anti-religious*, which is a belief system usually viewed as not itself being a religion. But if we look at what I described earlier, we can see that the content of a religion is, first, a belief in some certain way of thinking or ideology concerning the true nature of the world and humankind's place in it, and, second, action in accordance with that believed way of thinking or ideology. By this definition, we can see that anti-religion is itself clearly just a form of religion. In addition, such a way of thinking, because it intentionally seeks to deny the ideal, and because it seeks to remove the ideal from its importance and position in the real world, with a tendency to define the real as only those material phenomena and events which can be grasped and perceived by the eye and ear and the other physical sense organs, can be described as a viewpoint which places central importance upon, and that venerates, the *material*. It is a religion that worships the material.

Sekishin: Can there really be such religions?

Gudo: They exist now, as they have existed throughout human history. For example, in Greek philosophy, we find Thales, Anaximenes, Leucippus, Democritus and various others—the many thinkers who developed the schools of philosophy knows as materialism— who pursued matter as the basis of all that exists in the world. The ideas of those thinkers are usually put under the heading of philosophy, not religion, but my definition does not make much distinction between philosophy and religion. As I described earlier, if religion is belief in a unified way of thought concerning the nature of the world, combined with action in accordance therewith, then we see that we can also call these ideologies as themselves a type of religion, and that they can be called religions that place central importance upon, or venerate, the material.

16

Thereafter in the history of the Western World, we find the Middle Ages as a period manifesting an all-powerful Christianity, whereby the idealistic vision of Christianity was prevalent, and materialistic religions were out of favor. However, as we enter the Modern Age, we find the re-appearance of materialistic religions among the ideas of English Empiricism and of thinkers such as Francis Bacon and Hobbes. In the 19th Century, via Feuerbach, Marx and other materialists, religions placing importance upon the material became most strong.

Sekishin: So, Roshi … You think of Marxism as a religion?

Gudo: Yes I do. Its arising out of a belief that all that this world contains was born from a foundation in the physical and material, its construction of an intricate system of thought and ideology, and the efforts of its followers to reform society using, as a basis therefor, that system of thought and ideology … these can all be said to be clearly one type of religious behavior. I also believe that science can be a religion for some people to the extent that it is viewed … not merely as a tool for understanding aspects of this world in which we live … but as the *be all and end all* perspective for the way this world is, that nothing is true except as it has a basis in the material universe, seemingly harsh, cold and blindly operating … that, perhaps, the universe is nothing more than an equation, for example. It is not just a faith in the utility of Scientific Method (which I share, by the way), but a faith expounding that nothing has value, nothing really is true … be it love, poetic truth, artistic truth, the subjective truths of the heart … unless it can be tested and proven by Scientific Method. That is a perspective now too common in our world. Right or wrong, to the extent that such beliefs constitute a world-view, an ideology, to which people conform their lives … a faith in science is another religion.

Sekishin: So, which religions do you consider emphasize *action*? What do you mean by that?

Gudo: This refers to those religions that just call for us to be, to live and act here and now, while simultaneously accepting this world *as it is*, just as it is here and now, without appealing to some other world that is somehow better, more ideal. Because all such teachings ask of us is to be, to act here and now, in this very world in which we are living here and now, I call such philosophies religions of *action*. Buddhism is such

17

an existential religion. On the other hand, while Buddhism calls upon us to fully accept, to merely observe without judgment this world in which we are living, still, Buddhism need not be a philosophy of passivity. We need not but sit in bliss upon our lotus leaf, watching life pass us by. While fully accepting the world, while fully not wishing that the world were any other way than just the way it is, *simultaneously and from yet another perspective*, we are most free to act, live and choose as we think best, with wisdom and compassion. We need not be passive, but can live our lives abundantly, moving forward, all the while knowing that we are always just here, that there is no place ultimately to go other than where we are. In this way, it is a religion of action. And, again, equally important is the further perspective that in our acting, in our living, it is but the world which acts and lives as we act and live, for we are each but a facet of the world, an expression of the whole of reality without separation. In this stance, all concepts of subject and object are put aside, and our lives and the functioning of all reality constitute a single great activity, *one great functioning*. Thus, because we view the world as acting by and through each of us without separation or division, it is a religion of action. So, just being, living and acting is sacred, a sacred act, in and of itself. We can even try to better the world as best we can, while hand-in-hand recognizing the world as perfectly just what it is. Because we can live, must live and act even as we accept, so it is a religion of action.

I believe that religions of *action* are not included in the categories of religions that worship the *ideal* and those that focus on the *material*, but transcend both. I think that almost all of the world's religions fall into one or the other of the previously described categories. But, while their numbers are small, there do exist in this world religions not falling into one of those two categories, philosophies which can be said to transcend and swallow whole *both* the ideal and the material. Buddhism is an example. Buddhism possesses nothing within it equivalent to a god. Furthermore, it does not discount and reject the world of the physical, of the flesh. In fact, it honors the world we find before us. It does not recognize souls and spirits. Even if we just think alone about its characteristic of not denying or rejecting this actual world in which we live, we find that it is certainly not a religion that worships the ideal. On the other hand, if we think about it as a religion that seeks the ethical, warns against our drowning in the senses, which is a viewpoint that does not see the total of reality only in the empirical or physical, and which places importance on actions and seeks a unity of the objective and the subjective, Buddhism, from any viewpoint, is not a religion of the material. So, if we then ask what *is* the real centerpiece of the teachings of Buddhism, it is not the ideal, not the material, but in reality its central focus is the actions of human beings, *one's being and doing here and now.* When we encounter a religion such as Buddhism that places central importance on the actions of human beings here and now, that is called a religion which places highest value on *action*, a religion of action.

TEACHING IN JERUSALEM

THE CHOICE OF RELIGION

Sekishin: Are there any religions that do not fit into one of the three categories?

Gudo: There are not, in my opinion. These three categories are extremely inclusive and flexible, and I think it impossible to hypothesize a religion that is not included within the three categories.

Sekishin: So, does that mean that we each *must* choose one from among those three categories of religion?

Gudo: Yes, we must. At the start of our chat today, you said you know many people who boast of being without a religion. But someone who expresses a lack of belief in religion is, in fact, a person who has faith in an ideology of no religion. Such is an ideology too. If we were to place such a belief among the various categories we have been discussing, it would fall squarely into the category of a materialist religion.

Sekishin: If you put it that way, then it is not possible that there can be anyone who does not have a religion.

Gudo: That is right. At the very start of our discussion, you posed the question of whether or not, ultimately, religions are necessary, and that question can be answered in the way just described. All human beings, absent some psychological or pathological deficit, in some manner believe in one of the three types of religion described and have a world-view they act upon. It is therefore not a question of whether or not religion is necessary. Instead, the question is *which religion* among all possible religions we should choose. That is the ultimate limit and extent of the freedom that we human beings possess with regard to our religion.

II. AN AFFIRMATION OF THE REAL WORLD

THE WORLD *AS IT IS*

Sekishin: Roshi, thank you so much for explaining your thoughts on the nature of religion. Now, I would like to ask you to expand on your comments about Buddhism, and I would like to begin to discuss Buddhism more specifically. First, I would like to ask you about the most fundamental tenets of the religion known as Buddhism. If you were to express those tenets in only a few words, what would you say?

Gudo: If I were to express in a very few words the most fundamental tenets of Buddhism, I would have to say that Buddhism is an affirmation of the real world, a deep acceptance of the world *as it is*.

Sekishin: I see. But, I don't think I have ever heard it said before that way. What I thought, and what I have always heard, is that –quite the contrary– Buddhism developed as an ideology of great pessimism and rejection of the world. I have always thought that Buddhism's perspective is that this world we live in is but suffering, and that Buddhism seeks a way of escape from that suffering, and thus escape from this world.

Gudo: That is a common misunderstanding. So many people misunderstand Buddhism as being an ideology of pessimism. Before I had the opportunity first to read the writings of Master Dogen and to find out otherwise, I also thought vaguely that Buddhism was a religion of pessimism. But when I was fortunate to encounter Master Dogen's words, reading and re-reading such writings as the *Fukanzazengi*, the *Gakudoyojinshu*, the *Shobogenzo*, the *Eiheishingi* and the *Eiheikoroku*, and when I sought to systematically reconstruct the ideas that run through those writings, I found that the foundation of Buddhism as taught by Master Dogen is an *affirmation* of this real world, and of our human place in it. I was led to the firm belief that such an affirmation is to be found running all through his teachings. I was also led to the conviction that such an understanding of Buddhism is at the very core of all Buddhist ideology, running as a continuous link in its teachings from the very first, from the time of Gautama Buddha and thereafter.

Sekishin: What specifically led to the conclusion you describe?

Gudo: In the *Gakudoyojinshu*, Master Dogen states, *"Those who trust in the Buddha-Way must trust that the self is within the Way from the beginning, that we are free from confusion, upside-down ways of thinking, delusion, excesses or deficiencies, and mistakes."* Many of us incorrectly think of Buddhism as a religion whose principal point is the development within us of a consciousness of our deep fault and imperfection, of the iniquity present in human beings. And that through our faith or hard efforts, we can cast off and cleanse that fault, imperfection and iniquity. However, in Master Dogen's vision, a belief in Buddhism is a belief that we human beings are, from the very outset, from the very foundation, free of confusion, without need for reversal of values, that we are never deluded, nor deficient or burdened with excess; nor is there ever, ever any mistake.

Sekishin: I think I see. So, that kind of thinking is present in the teachings of Master Dogen… But, how is it that, as you say, such thinking is present running all through the history of Buddhism?

Gudo: Well, at first I also had some doubt about this. Thus, whenever I had the opportunity, I sought to study Buddhist writings and works other than those by Master Dogen. What I learned as a result is that, throughout the history of Buddhism, such thinking stands out most conspicuously, whether in the original early Buddhism as taught directly by Gautama Buddha, the early Buddhist schools and sects arising in the period centered on 200-100 BCE, and in Mahayana Buddhism as it arose during 100-300 CE.

For example, in the *Shobogenzo*, as a description of the scene in which Gautama Buddha attained realization, Master Dogen many times employs the expression, "*Myself, as well as this Earth which bears upon it myself, as well as each and all of the creatures alive which inhabit this Earth, are already but Truth.*" This is a depiction of the culminating moment of Gautama Buddha's six years of intense searching and practice whereby, while seated under the Bodhi Tree at Bodhgaya engaged in *Zazen*, he caught sight of the shining eastern star, and in that instant tasted the true nature of this world. Myself, as well as this Earth which bears upon it myself, as well as each and all of the creatures alive which inhabit this Earth, are already but Truth. This is a statement of the very moment of the Buddha's arrival at an affirmation of ultimate reality, of an observing and deep acceptance of this world as it is, just as it is.

Also, I am sure you know of one of the most important *sutras* of Mahayana Buddhism, the *Myo-Ho-Renge-Kyo*, the *Wonderful Dharma Lotus Flower Sutra*.

Sekishin: Yes, commonly known as the *Lotus Sutra*.

Gudo: Yes. In the *Lotus Sutra*, one important perspective representative of the central ideas of that *sutra* is the concept of *All Dharmas are Truth*.

Sekishin: What exactly does that mean, "All Dharmas are Truth?"

Gudo: In the phrase "All Dharmas are Truth", we find the term *All Dharmas*, which means all that really exists, all that exists which is this universe we live in. And *are Truth* means the appearance of Truth, that which exists as it is when seen without any of the preconceptions, biases or judgments that we usually bring with us. The things which are, *are* just what they are. In other words, the concept *All Dharmas are Truth* means that the actual condition, the true appearance of this very world in which we are living, is to be seen when viewed purely, with a quiet, pliant mind and an honest, yielding eye.

Related to this, we also see in the *Lotus Sutra* the frequent use of the term *nyoze*, meaning suchness, or *as-it-is-ness*, pointing to *this very reality*, the actual state of things that we are seeing right before our eyes. This is a very basic tenet of Buddhist belief.

In this way, we find in the philosophy of Buddhism that ... if we consider it deeply, but without a mind clinging too firmly to our own human judgments; if we try to accept the world just as-it-is without being insistent that the world be just as *we* each would want and demand from our small perspectives, from our own biases, hopes, dreams, likes and dislikes ... we find that, in actuality, this world is perfectly just what it is, an attitude which leads us right to a vision affirming this real world, things perfectly as-they-are.

Sekishin: If you put it that way, I can see that Buddhism contains many ideas affirming reality, this world just as-it-is.

Gudo: One phrase that has been at the nucleus of the philosophy of Buddhism since its most ancient origins is the phrase *nyojitsu-chiken*, "exactly perceiving reality." This too is a concept that teaches us that Buddhism looks upon this very world in which we live as just-as-it-is.

Sekishin: But on the other hand, Buddhism is thought of as teaching that all life is suffering, an ideology that says this world in which we live is a world of suffering, offering how we might free ourselves from that suffering through its practices.

Gudo: That is true. This very same Buddhism has been understood in a great variety of ways accompanying the many changes of history. So, it is true that there have been periods during which Buddhism has been explained as constituting, in fact, an extremely pessimistic belief system. However, if we look at the root origins of Buddhism—namely, if we think from the standpoint of what is commonly called early Buddhism, the early teachings by the founder of all Buddhism, Gautama Buddha himself—we can be sure that the most fundamental beliefs of Buddhism rest upon a solid foundation of thoroughgoing and deep *optimism*, a positive acceptance and profound sentiment of being right at home in this world, here and now. This life, this world, is *just-as-it-is*, not to be avoided, not to be escaped or fled.

DHARMA

Gudo: Let me try to explain, but from a somewhat different angle, the fact that Buddhism is at heart a teaching "affirming the real world" just "as it is." You already know, do you not, that among the precepts of Buddhism, the many traditional guidelines for conduct and right behavior by the followers of Buddhism, there is the precept of *Devotion to the Three Jewels*?

Sekishin: Yes, the *Three Jewels*, namely, the precept of devotion to *Buddha, Dharma and Sangha*. I believe that we receive this precept among the many precepts we undertake to abide by when we first commit to being Buddhists.

Gudo: That is right. Among those Three Jewels, the "Buddha" of *Devotion to Buddha* means the person who has realized truth, and refers specifically to Gautama Buddha. Therefore, the meaning is a devotion to the founder of Buddhism, to Gautama Buddha. Further, the "Sangha" of *Devotion to Sangha* is a word derived from the Sanskrit language of ancient India, and refers to the collective body of all Buddhists. Specifically, it points to the four traditional categories of Buddhist believers constituting the religious collective that is Buddhism, being namely the home leaving priests, both male and female, and the men and women who are home staying lay believers. In other words, Devotion to Sangha means devotion to this traditional body of followers of Buddhism.

Sekishin: I understand your explanation about Devotion to Buddha and Devotion to Sangha. But I think you omitted *Devotion to Dharma*, which comes right between those two?

Gudo: The explanation of Devotion to the Dharma can be a little long, so I have left it for the end. This word, *"Dharma,"* is located at the very heart of all the beliefs of Buddhism. It is said that a proper understanding of this word, of Dharma, is necessary as a gateway to a correct understanding of Buddhism itself.

Sekishin: Then, just what does Dharma mean?

Gudo: Dharma can have a few shades of meaning, distinctive yet not separate. As we can see from its usage in the many terms such as *Buddha Dharma*, the word "Dharma" has as one of its meanings the teachings of the Buddha, namely, the teachings of Gautama Buddha. It is the lessons that the Buddha expounded.

However, from a different perspective, Dharma also has such usages as *shohou*, meaning *all dharmas* or *all phenomena*, and *banbou*, meaning *the ten-thousand-things*, whereby Dharma, in these cases, means this actual world, the phenomena manifesting in the world, the reality of all that truly exists which surrounds us and upholds us in this world.

Accordingly, the word "Dharma" has at least two shades of meaning: the teachings of Gautama Buddha, namely, the order of the universe as explained by Gautama Buddha, and a meaning of that universe itself which surrounds us and sweeps us in. Dharma is the substantiality, that essence that provides us with those twin aspects of reality. Namely, the word Dharma stands for the teachings on the order of reality that we much uphold and maintain, as well as, simultaneously, that reality itself which upholds us and maintains us. Thereby, *Devotion to Dharma* is the precept of respect and veneration for the world of reality which is that order itself, that reality itself, as well as the precept which instructs us to study closely how best to act and behave in a manner impressed with and in keeping with that reality, and thereupon to act and behave in such ways.

THE MEANING OF RESPECT AND VENERATION OF REALITY

Sekishin: From your explanation so far, I am still a bit doubtful ... But I think I understand vaguely that the philosophy of Buddhism contains an aspect within it teaching respect and veneration for the world of reality, the world just as we find it.

But, is there really some value, some special merit as a way of thought, in a philosophy emphasizing a respect and veneration for reality in a manner like that?

Gudo: If we look from the perspective of Western thinking, which so much of the world is now raised with from the time we are young, we either are constantly holding up some ideal and are striving with all our might toward it; or, we are forced to give up such efforts when life thwarts our desires, when we are faced with a real situation before us which we cannot budge, whereupon we are forced to act as the real situation dictates although our heart is not in it, although it is against what we want. This is the way we humans tend to function when life does not meet our hopes and aspirations: first, ideals and hopes and dreams, then disappointment, retreat and resignation.

Accordingly, Buddhism offers a way of thinking that recognizes an absolute value in the real situation just *as it is* without resorting to ideals and hopes and dreams about how the world *should be*, and which studies the laws that rule this world of reality and encourages us to act in accordance with them. Although I do not want to say that such a way of thinking does not exist in Western thought, I believe it is still an extremely rare way of thinking.

Thus, I think your attitude is understandable when, so acclimated as we are to the typical Western ways of thinking as we have come to be, you have some doubt as to whether or not there is value in respecting and venerating that which is reality, in accepting life *just as it is.*

However, as I explained earlier, religions can be classified into three groups, with Buddhism as a religion that venerates *action* in the real world, here and now, just as it is. You can see that, between action and affirmation of the real world, there exists an intimate, fully inseparable relationship, and the belief system which is known as Buddhism is thus unique as a teaching, for it places at its center such action amid reality as it is.

Please understand that, to the extent that we do not change our viewpoint on the beliefs of Buddhism by taking the foregoing perspective as fundamental to it, Buddhism will always be left in apparent ambiguity and confusion, and will never become a truly comprehensible philosophy for us. Near the start of our conversation today, I touched upon the difficult nature of Buddhist philosophy, but the true cause of the difficulty found by some in Buddhist philosophy is a misunderstanding of the basic premises lying at the foundation of Buddhist philosophy: namely, a failure to see the special foundation of Buddhism in a respect and veneration of action amid reality just as it is. If we look from the viewpoint of Western thought, dividing ways of thinking into the stances of idealism and materialism, and if we wrongly assume that Buddhism is some form of idealism, wishing the world were some ideal way other than what it is, we are left with but a narrow understanding of Buddhism born from trying to grasp its tenets in that manner.

Quite the contrary, Buddhism is a school of thought based on realism, not leaning toward either idealism or materialism. Accordingly, unless you strive to understand Buddhism by fully taking to heart the basic principle that Buddhism is a way of thinking founded in realism, you will be unable to understand Buddhism even after thousands of years, tens of thousands of years of trying. On the other hand, if you do have the attitude that you will understand Buddhism as a school of *action-ism*, of realism, Buddhism will not be so hard to fathom, will not be some distant, mysterious, incomprehensible way of thought. It is but our acting, our living in this world, this checkered world filled with the greatest beauty and the most terrible ugliness, repugnant to the imaginary world we might wish for in our dreams. It is simply our life in this real world as we find it, our living and blossoming fully in this world, while accepting this world free from imagined longings, from dreams and cravings frustrated by circumstances that fail to meet our expectations.

III. THE MIDDLE WAY

WHAT IS THE "MIDDLE WAY?"

Sekishin: When I first heard from you, Roshi, that Buddhism is a religion affirming the real world, affirming reality just as-it-is, well, I found myself quite surprised at the statement, perhaps because I had never heard it put that way before. I very much doubted the idea. Somehow, I had thought of Buddhism as offering an escape from this world to some other reality. But what you said has started to make sense to me, and I feel much more convinced by it.

Gudo: That is not unexpected. You see, Buddhism's basic religious principal affirming reality *as-it-is* became blurred and confused at an early point in its history, and, because of this, Buddhism came to be ambiguous in meaning and uncertain in its tenets over some two thousand and several hundred years. Moreover, it came to be generally regarded as a religion that is very difficult, or even impossible to understand.

Sekishin: Alright … If we put aside for the moment our discussion of Buddhism's basic principal as its affirmation of reality, please discuss some other principals important in understanding Buddhism.

Gudo: Well, there are any number of important principals. One that I must discuss, I would think, is the principal of *The Middle Way*.

Sekishin: Ah, yes, "The Middle Way," "The Four Noble Truths," "The Law of the Twelve Causes," "The Eightfold Path," these are among the most commonly cited fundamental principles of Early Buddhism, are they not? It is that "Middle Way" to which you refer, I take it.

Gudo: Yes it is. It is the teaching of the "Middle Way" found in Early Buddhism, at the root of all Buddhist philosophy as a teaching given by Gautama Buddha himself.

Sekishin: I must confess that, sometimes when I hear the expression "middle way," I feel a bit of instinctive revulsion, as if it means, just make a lukewarm effort, or just take the safe and sure road, or just have a compromising attitude about life. It gives me that halfhearted kind of feeling.

LECTURE AT THE TOKEI-IN TEMPLE

Gudo: Certainly, among some people who hear the words "middle way," perhaps especially among young people, there is a spirit of resistance toward any idea that seems on first impression to imply a weak indecisiveness toward life. They are not to be blamed for their misunderstanding, I think. Even in my case, when I was young, I felt that Buddhism's doctrine of the Middle Way must imply some passive spirit of tepid concession or compromise toward life, and I really could not understand its meaning. As I grew older, however, and as my understanding of Buddhism deepened, I began to feel very, very strongly the important place in Buddhist philosophy occupied by the concept of the Middle Way, and that, to the extent the true meaning of

32

the Middle Way is not fully grasped, the true meaning of Buddhism cannot be fully grasped.

Sekishin: If that is the case, please tell me about the real meaning of the Middle Way.

Gudo: Because the meaning of the Middle Way indicates a path right between something and something else, the first question to address is the nature of those somethings.

Sekishin: So, to say it most directly, it means the Middle Way between two extremes.

Gudo: The extremes which the concept of the Middle Way anticipates are not only of a single type. However, if we ask, historically, what Gautama Buddha first meant when he spoke of "the Middle Way" in his own day and culture, he meant that path standing between the extremes of Brahmanism and the extremes of what are known as *The Teachings of the Six Non-Buddhist Masters*.

Sekishin: Let us discuss all of that. Let us begin with Brahmanism. What is that?

Gudo: Commencing from around the period 1,200 - 1,000 BCE, a folkloric tradition was handed down widely in ancient India, a tradition now known to us through the sacred books called the Vedas. The content of these Vedas is representative of the religious thinking prevalent in Indian culture at that time. From around 800 BCE there also developed, arising out of the Vedas, a philosophical statement known as the Upanishads.

In the process of orally handing down the Vedas and the Upanishads from generation to generation, their transmission gave birth to a certain dominant social caste known as the Brahmans. That Brahmic caste was held high by the ordinary population as the social group blessed most by the gods, and based thereon, they came to form the senior caste in the social structure of ancient India. Thereupon, the religion advocated by the Brahman caste, centered upon the ideas of the Vedas and the Upanishads and other sources, became Brahmanism.

Sekishin: What were the central tenets of Brahmanism?

Gudo: Well, the content of both the Vedas and the Upanishads is not something that clear and simple that it can be summarized in a few words, at least not without the greatest risk in doing so. That being said, if I were to attempt to briefly summarize the central concepts of the Upanishads, I would say:

(1) This world in which we live was formed by a Creator, usually called "Brahma;"

(2) Accordingly, it can also be said that this world is an entity ruled by Brahma;

(3) Within the heart of each human being is a self called "atman", this atman being an aspect of Brahma;

(4) Accordingly, we human beings can achieve happiness by actualizing and realizing the atman within us, thereby unifying with Brahma; and

(5) Even after the death of the physical body, the atman can be reborn in the world of Brahma.

Sekishin: So, when we think about the fact that Brahmanism recognizes a creator, that it speaks of an inner spirit named the "atman," and of a world after death, I feel that this belief system would fall, among the three categories of religions you discuss, in the category of idealistic religions.

Gudo: Yes, that is so. If we were to place Brahmanism among the three categories of religion, it is a religion that venerates the ideal.

Sekishin: All right. Then, what are *The Teachings of the Six Non-Buddhist Masters*?

Gudo: The "Teachings of the Six Non-Buddhist Masters" refers to six teachers of six schools considered heretical from the standpoint of Buddhist thought. It means the teachings of these six thinkers, described by the Buddha in the early Buddhist scriptures as falling outside the teachings of Buddhism.

Sekishin: Who were these six thinkers?

Gudo: The six thinkers were individuals active during the age of Gautama Buddha, or shortly prior thereto. Their names are Sañjaya-velatthiputta, Ajita-kesakambarin, Makkhali-gosāla, Purāna-kassapa, Pakudha-kaccāyana and Nigantha-nātaputta.

Sekishin: Which doctrines did each of these six teachers propose?

Gudo: Each of these six thinkers criticized the ideas of Brahmanism in some way, and proposed a philosophy in contrast to it. Accordingly, in contrast to Brahmanism, we can say that they tended to be upholding doctrines which, in the three categories of religion, can be categorized as either religions of materialism or as religions of action.

Let us begin with Sañjaya-velatthiputta, who claimed that debate and dispute is meaningless with regard to those problems about which human beings cannot reach a conclusion, and that, foregoing such disputation, it is best to engage in practices and ascetic training for the purpose of understanding.

Ajita-kesakambarin was a sensual materialist, who philosophized that the purpose of life is to be found in pleasure.

Makkhali-gosāla, a fatalist, denied the existence of free will as well as the meaningfulness of effort on the part of human beings.

Purāna-kassapa denied the reality of values such as good and evil, and therefore rejected the significance of morality.

Pakudha-kaccāyana professed a materialist theory, denied morality and asserted a philosophy of hedonism.

Nigantha-nātaputta, the founder of Jainism, divided this world into the spiritual and the material, advocating a control and suppression of the material, and an uplifting of the spiritual.

Sekishin: How would the three categories of religion apply in each case?

Gudo: The four thinkers Ajita-kesakambarin, Makkhali-gosāla, Purāna-kassapa and Pakudha-kaccāyana are clearly believers in materialistic religions. However, with regard to Sañjaya-velatthiputta and Nigantha-nātaputta, the situation is not so clear. To categorize their ideas, it can be said that they were intoning religions placing value upon action, but perhaps because the thought structure of their systems was not sufficiently clear and precise in comparison to Buddhism, they were subject to criticism by Gautama Buddha.

Sekishin: So, the concept of "the Middle Way" as expressed in Buddhism means the Middle Way between the extremes of Brahmanism and the extremes of The Teachings of the Six Non-Buddhist Masters. Therefore, if we were to summarize the point, does the Middle Way mean the middle path between religions of materialism and religions of idealism, namely, a religion placing importance on action?

Gudo: That is right. The intent of Gautama Buddha in putting forth the Middle Way was to point to the fact that Brahmanism was in error, and that The Six Teachers were in error as well. Therefore, if we try to boil it down, he was asserting that the ways of thinking of materialistic religions are in error and, no less, the ways of thinking of idealistic religions are in error.

AFFIRMATION OF REALITY & THE MIDDLE WAY

Sekishin: However, if you are going to assert that idealistic religions are in error and that materialistic religions are also in error, and if you are going to assert that a religion of action is superior to each, you had better have some grounds for arguing so. Isn't that right?

Gudo: That is exactly right. However, the difficult point is that the problem of which religion a person should choose is fundamentally a question having its roots in most people's actual life circumstances ahead of any logic or theory. Therefore, it is not possible to make a simplistic, logical demonstration that, for example, among some three religions A, B & C, for some reason C is clearly *the* religion which is best and proper. It is not that I avoid a good debate, or that I don't have confidence in my own opinions, but that a problem such as the choosing of one's religion, a problem that generally touches upon the very foundations of life and its meaning, is really a problem that finds its solution at a level of the heart more basic or prior to logical or theoretical discussion. It is not to be solved by piling up logical debate on the issue, but is to be solved at a gut level by the piling up of long years of personal life experience, by wavering back and forth on the question any number of times until, gradually and naturally, one's own beliefs become clear and sure.

Sekishin: So, Roshi, by what road did you personally come to a belief in Buddhism?

Gudo: Well, one of the main causes of my developing faith in Buddhism has been that, in the course of the circumstances of my own life, I came to appreciate to a terrible degree the pain and ineffectiveness inherent in efforts and striving based on idealism. It is very common that people, especially when they are young, tend toward very idealistic thinking. However, our ideals—meaning the longings and desires conceived within our hearts that life and circumstances *should be* this way or *should be* that way—are not necessarily realized and achieved in the real world.

Quite the contrary, it is usually the case that the ideals we hold will be in discord and at loggerheads with reality, and life will toss a cold bucket of water on our hopes and dreams. To the extent that we are faithful to our ideals, we will suffer at the hands of the contradictions and inconsistencies between the ideal and the actual state of life, and we will agonize in our efforts to force the two to be in accord. Certainly, the undertaking of great efforts in pursuit of some high goal enlivens and kindles our human existence, allows us to feel what is often called a reason to live, or a goal in life. I am not saying, by any means, that one should abandon one's goals in favor of becoming uncaring, disinterested, without ideals. But is it the case that human beings must stake our happiness on the pursuit of ideals which, in so many cases, are doomed to fail and which will eventually force us to quit? This was the doubt that I developed regarding idealistic philosophy as a result of engaging in childish struggle and striving over long years in my own life.

Sekishin: So, I would think that, usually, a belief in a materialistic "realism" would be born in response.

Gudo: Yes. But you just called it materialistic *realism*. From the standpoint of Buddhism, that is not correct. It is quite commonly thought in modern society that a veneration of the material, so-called "materialism," is the same as "realism." For example, that science, and a vision of a universe consisting of but cold, dark, meaningless matter, is the last word on what is real. However, such a stance is not supported in Buddhism. From a Buddhist standpoint, matter is nothing more than an abstract concept representing that which can be grasped with our senses. It is not the same as reality.

Sekishin: So, what you are saying is that in Buddhism, reality—or to put it in other words, Dharma—signifies that state of being which is itself neither the ideal nor the material?

Gudo: Yes. The placing of importance on reality found in the thinking of Buddhism does not lean toward the ideal, does not lean toward the material. Accordingly, thus comes the meaning of *the Middle Way*. Buddhism, through its use of the term *Dharma* in its true meaning of not the ideal, not the material, thereby grasps the real world. Thereupon, it places complete trust and faith in this world of reality, namely, in that which is Dharma.

You said at the outset, Sekishin, that sometimes when you hear the expression "the Middle Way" you feel as if it means a lukewarm effort, just to take the safe and sure road, or just to have a compromising attitude about life, a weak indecisiveness toward life. But to the contrary, Buddhism, much as idealism itself, lets us know that we are fully capable of pursuing high goals which might enliven and kindle our human existence, any goal in life available to us. I have had personal goals in my studies, work and family growing up that were important to realize. We have large goals and small goals, such as my simple goal each day just to dress and tie the strings on my priest's robes, and humankind must always have grand goals to make this world better that we must never forsake.

But the difference with idealism is that, simultaneously and hand-in-hand with our moving forward, from a parallel perspective not separate therefrom, we accept, right to the marrow, this world *as it is*, perfectly what it is with all that may be taken as imperfection; our world of *perfect imperfection* which we can always strive to improve, yet simultaneously is always just as it is. While fully accepting the world, while fully not wishing that the world were any other way than just the way it is, we are most free to act, to live and choose as we think best. We need not be passive, but can live our lives abundantly. That stance of moving forward, fully living life, while simultaneously knowing that there is no place else ever to go, that is the the Middle Way.

TYING ON OF ROBES

39

IV. THE FOUR NOBLE TRUTHS

A NEW WAY TO SEE "THE FOUR NOBLE TRUTHS."

Sekishin: So, can it be said that Buddhism is a way of thinking that supplants and rejects both idealism and materialism?

Gudo: Yes. From one perspective, we can say that it is exactly that. On the other hand, and from a complementary perspective, Buddhism also embraces, transcends and fully contains within its structure *both* idealistic thinking *and* materialistic thinking.

Sekishin: How does it accomplish that hard trick?

Gudo: Well, the philosophical system within Buddhism that allows such an accomplishment is the system we call "The Four Noble Truths."

Sekishin: Ah… That is the Buddhist teaching containing the four concepts saying, first, this life is a life of suffering, that the cause of that suffering is our craving and desire, that suffering can be brought to an end through the elimination of craving and desire, and finally, that the so-called "Eightfold Path" is the means to the end of suffering …

Gudo: That is right. Those four propositions are known as "The Four Noble Truths," and are rightly said to be among the most important elements constituting the philosophy of Buddhism. After Gautama Buddha attained truth under the Bodhi Tree at Magadha, his very first teaching, spoken to the five ascetics who had been his former companions, was an imparting of these Four Noble Truths. Gautama Buddha himself asserted the centrality within Buddhism of these Four Noble Truths, and there is no doubt as to their great importance.

Sekishin: Well, hmmm, I don't think that life is all just suffering. When I hear this, I doubt very much just how accurate these Noble Truths really are. For example, the First Noble Truth, namely, that *this world is suffering*, is that correct? Of course, this human life we all live will contain much pain and suffering sometimes. However, life is not necessarily all suffering. For example, when we drink and celebrate happy times, when we enjoy a good day with our friends, when we have had some success or achievement in our work, or when we fall in love and get married, when our children succeed in their lives before our eyes… Do we really have to grimace at it all and think of these nice things as being the cause of suffering?

I understand that, well, even pleasure is the root of suffering when we become attached to the pleasure, or crave and desire the pleasure to excess. Still, when we look at the Second Noble Truth, which says that the cause of all suffering in this world is our craving and desire, is such a cut and dried statement really correct too? Is that all it is? Isn't the picture a bit more complex, and the causes of human suffering manifold?

And even if so, with regard to the assertion that suffering can be brought to an end through the elimination of craving and desire, which is the Third Noble Truth, I just don't think it possible for a human being, by our basic nature, to be able to totally eliminate desire and such within us. I do not think it possible or even optimal for us to become desireless and passionless like cold automatons. Only a cold and lifeless stone is without all desire and passion, and I do not think that the goal of our Buddhist practice is to become like lifeless stones. Accordingly, I just cannot think well of some "Eightfold Path" or other strange concept that seeks to force us into forms of behavior which are unnatural or even impossible for normal human beings. Is the idea that our true and good inner nature will manifest somehow by the mere cutting off of our desire? I very, very much doubt it.

Gudo: Well, I think your doubts are right to an extent. I too have wrestled with great misgivings having connection to the manner in which The Four Noble Truths typically have been explained and taught.

Sekishin: But, Roshi, did you not just say that The Four Noble Truths form one of the centerpieces of Buddhist philosophy?

TRADITIONAL IMAGE OF BUDDHA TEACHING

Gudo: Oh, yes, I believe that The Four Noble Truths are among the most important foundations for the wisdom of Buddhism. However, at the same time, and so that The Four Noble Truths can rightly occupy their central place in Buddhism, I believe that it is necessary for us to somewhat revise the way in which The Four Noble Truths have been commonly explained. I feel we should find the deeper meaning in these truths. I would like to propose an alternative perspective on The Four Noble Truths that may help illuminate the real wisdom they contain.

Sekishin: But, I believe that the description I gave earlier of the content of The Four Noble Truths is the prevalent description as set forth in several very ancient *suttas*, and I think that it is consistent with the authoritative explanation.

Gudo: That is certainly true, and that is one perspective on the teaching. But, we must keep in mind that even such extremely ancient writings as the oldest Pali *suttas* were not ultimately set down until some hundreds of years or more after the death of Gautama Buddha. Such time allowed for various interpretations to develop with regard to the basic teachings. If we were, for example, to think backwards from our present year... subtracting a hundred years would place us near the start of the

43

twentieth century, and two hundred years would take us back to the time of Napoleon. So, when we think about how impossible it is for us who are alive today to imagine just how life was a century ago... Of course, we can know a bit from reading books or from paintings and photographs and such, but it is almost impossible for us to guess the reality of people's feelings and experiences in their day-to-day lives, the realities of food, clothing and shelter, the actual social environment and the like. And we are left just so much more at a loss with regard to imagining the situation some two centuries ago.

If we think from such a standpoint, in Gautama Buddha's day, which lacked the methods of accurately recording and transmitting ideas that we now possess in our time, the passing of a hundred or two hundred years would have caused much loss—perhaps more than we can even imagine—in the attempt to properly and accurately transmit the teachings. That is so even if a rigorous system of oral recitation and repetition were employed, as is claimed for the Buddha's words that were passed down orally for hundreds of years. Accordingly, the content of even the oldest of *suttas* and other sources just cannot be said to be always fully and necessarily reflecting the real thinking of Gautama Buddha.

Sekishin: So, Roshi, what you are saying is that you have some doubt as to whether the explanation of The Four Noble Truths found in the old *suttas* and other sources is the real meaning intended by Gautama Buddha, and that other perspectives might help bring out the wisdom in the teaching...?

Gudo: That is right. You said before that you have a hard time believing the explanation regarding The Four Noble Truths as found in many traditional sources. Well, since the explanation found in the old *suttas* and such was created based upon an oral retelling and reciting from memory passed down from teller to teller for hundreds of years after the lifetime of Gautama Buddha, a long period during which every single person who had had the experience of actually seeing Gautama Buddha, of hearing his teachings directly, gradually died off, well, we should not over-value these books unquestioningly just because they are ancient, and we can look at these matters in other ways.

Sekishin: In that case, Roshi, what is your other understanding of The Four Noble Truths?

Gudo: As you said, the most common manner of understanding of The Four Noble Truths has been that: (1) this life is suffering, (2) the cause of that suffering is craving and desire, (3) and, if we were but to cut off craving and desire (4) the true and proper human state would manifest. The Eightfold Path is the way. However, such a manner of understanding, such an interpretation of this actual world in which we live, is just too simplistic, too dogmatic. By approaching this in another manner, we can better bring the teaching to life. It is not that I am saying that the traditional interpretations are wrong. Rather, I hope to explain them in a way that looks to their implications from other perspectives to shed light on the real meaning of desire, suffering and the cure for suffering.

WITH ZEN STUDENTS IN CHILE

First, in the very phrase *The Four Noble Truths*, the meaning of *Truths* as used therein, as shown by its usage in *Noble Truths* or in other Buddhist terminology such as *The Truth of the First Principle* (Jap: *daiichigitai*), is not meant merely the ordinary meaning of the "truth" of some determination or decision, e.g., the truth that *something* is determined to be *something*, that X = Y or 1+1 = 2. Instead, it should be understood as a word pointing to several bases of thinking serving as foundations underlying all decision making.

Namely, if we put it into modern terms, "Truths" is a word expressing several fundamental or basic standpoints or viewpoints, such as would be conveyed in the expressions "life views" or "worldviews." Accordingly, the meaning of *The Truth of Suffering* (Jap: *kutai*) means a way of thinking centered on suffering, *The Truth of Accumulation or Aggregation* (*shutai* in Japanese) means a way of thinking centered on accumulations and aggregates, *The Truth of Self-Regulation* (Jap: *mettai*) means a way of thinking centered on self-control and self-regulation, and *The Truth of the True Way* (Jap: *dotai*) means a way of thinking centered on the True Way.

Sekishin: I do not think that I have heard The Four Noble Truths expressed in this way before. So, Roshi, are you saying that The Four Noble Truths constitute, in fact, a list of four separate and independent ways of thinking?

Gudo: Yes. From another perspective, I believe that Gautama Buddha's true meaning was just that. They are separate and independent ways of thinking, yet fit and build, one upon the other, in a unified and settled order which constitutes a characteristic and distinctive perspective of Buddhism. The Chinese characters which were chosen by the early translators of Buddhist literature to express the Sanskrit words *catvary aryasatyani* are pronounced *shi sho tai* in Japanese. *Shi* means four, *sho* means sacred or noble, and *tai* means truth or philosophy. Often, however, they are referred to as *shi tai ron*, wherein *ron* means theory. Thus the phrase The Theory of Four Philosophies can also be used as quite a close translation. The word *satya* in Sanskrit has arrived in Japanese as *tai*. Both *satya* and *tai* can be interpreted in several ways; although the prime meaning of both is undoubtedly "truth," the word "philosophy" is also an accurate rendering from the Japanese.

Sekishin: All right. What, then, do you mean when you say that *The Truth of Suffering* means a way of thinking centered on suffering?

Gudo: If we start with The Truth of Suffering, we find that in the old *suttas* and in other sources, there is an explanation of the so-called *Four Sufferings and Eight Sufferings*, which I believe serves as a good point of reference. The Four Sufferings are birth, old age, sickness and death, and the Eight Sufferings are the first four sufferings, plus the sufferings of being apart from those one loves, meeting those one detests, not obtaining one's desires, and sufferings arising from the five aggregates. Put another way, among these Eight Sufferings is the suffering of being unable to escape from the desire to be together with those one loves, the suffering of being unable to fulfill one's desire not to encounter persons one loathes, the suffering of not being able to obtain that which one wishes to obtain, and the suffering of longing for quiet and stillness though being unable to realize quiet and stillness, and others. Each is a suffering born from the inability of human beings to realize and achieve the longings and desires we carry in our hearts.

In addition, The Four Sufferings of birth, old age, sickness and death represent an inability to attain a desired happiness during life. For example, we cannot escape the yearning for health and youth, although such cannot always be the case. We cannot live forever, or escape from death, although we might hope to do so. Each suffering is born from our inability to escape the longings and desires we each carry with us, an inability to accept life as it is. Each stems from our desire that life be some other way; it is our creation of idealized dreams of how we would otherwise wish life to be, how life should be, other than just what it is as we find it.

These longings, desires, wishes and such represent our dissatisfaction with the world as it is, and a dream of how we wish circumstances would be or should be to make us happy, We have a vision of an ideal life, a notion of what would make us happy once and for all *if only* it would come to be. *Dukkha*, suffering, may perhaps be better translated as dissatisfaction with how things are. That is, it is the suffering that necessarily arises in idealism, in idealistic thinking. The idealistic concept is always much better than the checkered world as we find it, here and now. So, it is not that the denial of a desire must necessarily result in suffering, but that idealistic philosophies and views have, inherent within themselves, a characteristic of suffering. In contrast, in Buddhism, which allows us to be content and fully at home in the world just as it is, and amid circumstances just as we find them, while *simultaneously* holding all the dreams and desires of an active life, in Buddhism, we might feel the sting of a desire denied to us, yet, in our simultaneous equanimity and acceptance of that fact, we merely observe, with objectivity and tranquility, the throb of the hard punch that life may have handed to us. There may be some pain, some sadness perhaps, but true suffering can occur only when we cling to the pain, wrap our minds around it, and refuse to observe it all from a tranquil stance of acquiescence. We may dream that the path of life would take us to the north, and we work *step-by-step* to travel north toward our goal. But, when life blocks our path, when the wind blows us onto a southern course, the Buddhist will accept that fact, will appraise the altered circumstances of life and plot a new route, a new direction, *step-by-step*.

I do not believe that the Buddha held that sickness, old age and death are the cause of suffering in and of themselves. Rather, he discovered that our refusal to embrace and allow sickness, old age and death, and to cling to and crave health, youth and life in their stead as our desired ideal, is the root of suffering. Dukkha, dissatisfaction, arises from sickness, but only when we refuse the condition; from old age, if we long for youth; in encountering death, because we cling to life; by loss, when we cannot let go; due to violated expectations, because we wished otherwise.

So, if we look from such a standpoint, we can understand that suffering is linked to our inability as human beings to realize our inner ideals and, looking at it from the opposite standpoint, that a way of thinking centered on suffering means a way of thinking centered upon the ideals which are the cause of suffering. Specifically, suffering is a reaction to our desired ideals whereby life fails, from our subjective viewpoint, to meet the artificial standards, hopes, wishes, dreams and expectations we self-righteously place upon it within our human hearts. Accordingly, The Truth of Suffering can be understood to refer to ways of thinking having as their center-point human desire for the ideal, and thus is an expression bearing the flavor of the philosophies of idealism as found in ancient India.

Sekishin: And, so, what is the second of the four, *The Truth of Accumulation or Aggregation* as a way of thinking centered on accumulations and aggregates?

Gudo: In some old *suttas* and *sutras*, this is sometimes referred to as the Truth of Cause, and there are many examples of this cause being interpreted to mean the cause that is desire. However, in other examples, this cause is interpreted as being the cause displayed in cause and effect relationships, another central concept in Buddhism, and I believe that such an interpretation may be closer to an original meaning intended by

Gautama Buddha. This latter perspective can also cast light on the true significance of the teaching.

Thus, in place of the "Truth of Cause," I prefer the term "The Truth of Accumulation" or "Aggregation," which I believe is closer to the original Sanskrit word, *samdaya*. If we try to restate this "cause" as the "cause" of *"cause and effect"* then, using other words, we might say it means, for example, the causal relationships existing among the accumulations and aggregations of particles and forces of physical matter, the physical phenomena that constitute this objective world, which surrounds and includes us. We can understand The Truth of Accumulation or Aggregation to mean the causes and interactions found in the physical matter of this objective world of which we are part, and material causes as the causes found in cause and effect relationships in this world. This Truth can be thus called the The Truth of Aggregates, meaning the aggregates of matter, the Truth of the cause and effect relationships of the aggregates of matter in the objective world that surround us.

Sekishin: When you say matter, it thus seems opposite to the idealistic thinking of The Truth of Suffering.

Gudo: That is correct. If we say that The Truth of Suffering bears the flavor of the philosophies of idealism of ancient India, then I believe that Gautama Buddha's real meaning in The Truth of Aggregates is materialism, the philosophies of materialism of ancient India. As the Buddha taught, falling one-sidedly into a materialistic viewpoint, and holding as too important the experiences of our senses, is also—just as with idealism—a way of thinking that is a source of suffering. We have to keep in mind that Gautama Buddha did not view the real world as a world of only pure physical matter lacking all meaning and value, as something cold and dead and meaningless. To see life and the world as, at heart, nothing but a collection of physical phenomena, this is too a source of suffering and delusion.

Sekishin: What, then, is the next of the four, *The Truth of Self-Regulation*? You describe this as a way of thinking centered on self-control and self-regulation …

Gudo: The term in Sanskrit is *nirodha-satya*, which also can be translated as The Truth of Negation or The Truth of Synthesis. I have sometimes thought such terms to be a good translation, for the meaning of this Truth of "Negation" and of "Synthesis" is the negation and synthesis of the ideal, the negation and synthesis of the material. To the extent that we human beings are living in a world centered on what we think, what we wish and dream, our thoughts, wishes and dreams, and our ideals, will be a cause of problems to us. And to the extent that we human beings are living in a world in which we are wrapped up in the material and what we experience through the senses, we shall revere one-sidedly the material and hold as overly important our senses. However, besides the worlds of thinking and of the senses, besides the perspectives of the ideal and the material, one additional, most important perspective exists for human beings: this is the world of *action*, of being and doing which accepts the world just as it is. It is the world that sweeps in and swallows whole *both* the ideal and the material, right here and now. It is called a world of action because this world is active now, is acting here and now, and we exist now, are acting here and now as an expression of that active world.

LECTURE AT TIBETAN BUDDHIST CENTER IN BELGIUM

Therefore, because this world of action is, at this very moment, existentially the world of the present moment, there is no time to slowly contemplate this or that, nor time to confirm phenomena sensually. The world of action is a world in which ideas and ideals are negated, transcended, synthesized and absorbed, and simultaneously, a world in which matter and the senses are negated, transcended, synthesized and absorbed. It is the world that is this present moment in time, the world which, spatially, embodies this very place: here and now. It is a way of thinking that transcends thinking, as well as a way of thinking that transcends the senses. The philosophy born out of a world of action, possessing such a meaning both negating and absorbing each of the ideal and the material, can thus be called *The Truth of Negation* or *The Truth of Synthesis*.

Sometimes it is referred to as *The Truth of Extinction*, perhaps meaning some ultimate extinction of thought, extinction of the senses or extinction of all desire. But I do not prefer that term. Nothing is made extinct, and even desire is still there as a necessary aspect of our being alive as human beings. But all is gone beyond, embraced and synthesized into a whole. Because—more than any true eradicating and extinguishing of the ideal and material— it sweeps in and swallows whole both the ideal and the material. So we had best not call it The Truth of Extinction.

However, the Sanskrit word *nirodha* can have a variety of meanings, such as confinement, locking up, imprisonment, to restrain, check, control, and so forth. For this reason, I think that we also might say that *nirodha* can mean a form of self-control, or self-regulation. In order to realize that state of action in which ideas and ideals are negated, transcended, synthesized and absorbed, and simultaneously, in which matter and the senses are negated, transcended, synthesized and absorbed, a state in which we live in the world as it is, just here and now, what we must realize is a state of balance in body, balance in mind, a regulation of body and mind.

One subject that we will have a chance to discuss later in detail concerns the various physical and mental effects of *Zazen*, such as the effect of *Zazen* upon the human autonomic nervous system, which is brought into a state of balance, and the regulation of the body and mind brought into a state of balance. Thus, I now prefer to describe this The Truth of Self-Regulation, as a way of thinking centered on self-control and self-regulation realizing balance in body, balance in mind. By The Truth of the True Way, and most specifically, by the practice of *Zazen*, we are brought into that state in which body and mind are balanced, controlled and regulated in such a way, and The Truth of Self-Regulation thereby attained. So, this is the The Truth of Self-

Regulation, The Truth of Self-Control, and perhaps we might also term it The Truth of Equilibrium for this balance and equilibrium of body and mind.

Sekishin: This leads us to *The Truth of the True Way*, the Truth centered on the True Way.

Gudo: The True Way is a translation from the original Sanskrit, *marga-satya*, and is said to encompass the true teachings of the Buddha. We said that the thinking behind The Truth of Self-Regulation is a way of thinking pertaining to the world of action, which calls upon us to realize a state of balance in body, balance in mind in our living. But that does not mean that, naturally and in and of themselves, each and every one of our actions will be so balanced, right and proper at all times or in all circumstances. Accordingly, our actions and behavior are sometimes balanced, right and proper, and sometimes unbalanced. But that state in which they are in accord and agreement with the balanced state is best understood as being The True Way. In the *suttas*, this Truth of the True Way is explained in its connection to *The Eightfold Path*, which is not just by coincidence.

The Eightfold Path consists of True View, True Thinking, True Speech, True Action, True Livelihood, True Effort, True Consciousness and True Balance. These call for us to engage in and hold proper and balanced viewpoints, proper and balanced ideas, proper and balanced manners of speaking, proper and balanced conduct, proper and balanced ways of living, proper and balanced courses of endeavor, proper and balanced states of mind and proper and balanced states of body. When each of these types of personal actions and behaviors are in a state of perfect balance, such is what we call The True Way.

However, realizing and achieving such states of balance is not an easy thing. For this reason, Gautama Buddha urged the practice of *Zazen* as the means giving rise *instantaneously* to that state of perfect balance, harmony and accord between our actions and the balance, rightness and propriety which is the order of the universe. Accordingly, The Truth of the True Way, if we examine its meaning thoroughly, can also be said to be that way of living centered upon the practice of *Zazen*.

THE FOUR NOBLE TRUTHS AND THE *SHOBOGENZO.*

Sekishin: I would like to focus on *Zazen* a bit later, Roshi, and discuss it then in depth. For now, Roshi, may I ask on what basis you came to adopt the interpretation of The Four Noble Truths that you have just put forth?

Gudo: That is directly related to the many, many years that I have spent reading and considering Master Dogen's *Shobogenzo.*

Sekishin: Is the same explanation of The Four Noble Truths found in the *Shobogenzo*?

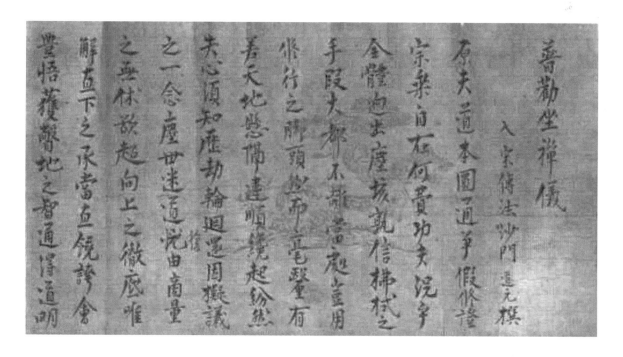

FUKANZAZENGI IN MASTER DOGEN'S HAND

Gudo: There is no explanation that directly maps out such a structure, or which speaks in exactly those words. Yet, throughout the *Shobogenzo* there appears again and again a logic and method of assertion attempting to explain this world of reality in which we live by means of the multi-layered and complex usage and interworking of four ways of thinking, which, although seemingly in conflict with each other, fit and build, one

53

upon the other, in a unified and settled order, and which constitute a characteristic and distinctive perspective of Buddhism.

Through the combination of those four ways of thinking, a fine explanation is afforded of this world of reality. And to the extent that we do not employ this unique combination of the four ways of thinking, I feel keenly that a good explanation of this strange and complex, multi-layered world of reality in which we live must elude us. I therefore came to the hypothesis that The Four Noble Truths as expounded by Gautama Buddha within early Buddhism, and that method of assertion which combines and interweaves the four ways of thinking as appears again and again throughout the *Shobogenzo*, are one and the same.

Master Dogen expresses his ideas in the *Shobogenzo* based on a pattern of four phases. First, he explains a problem from the idealistic point of view; that is, as an idea using abstract concepts. Then, immediately after this first phase, he explains the same problem, but this time from the objective, or materialistic point of view. In other words, he gives concrete examples and facts. In the next phase, he explains the problem yet a third time as a real problem; that is, from the perspective of the philosophy of action. Of course, he cannot explain the reality surrounding the problem merely with words in a book, but he does so by bringing together the subjective, idealistic viewpoint which he presents first, and the second objective, materialistic viewpoint, via a viewpoint merging and transcending idea and matter, the subjective and objective as an unbroken whole, which is reality. This is the standpoint of a philosophy of action. He synthesizes the two viewpoints into a realistic appraisal of the issue: an unbroken synthesis of the self and the external world. And in the final phase—since words alone will not suffice in a description of reality—he tries to suggest the subtle, ineffable nature of reality itself by using symbolic, poetic or figurative forms of speech.

After I had read and re-read Master Dogen's book, I became used to this unique way of thinking about things. He discusses all problems from three points of view, subjective and ideal, objective and material, and realistic action. He then goes on to insist on the difference between his three viewpoints and the real situation itself beyond mere descriptive words. Using this method, he is able to explain the reality of a situation clearly and logically. He believes that the most important thing is to experience what reality itself is, just as it is; at the same time, he realizes how impossible this is using the medium of the written word alone.

When I remembered The Four Noble Truths, which at first had defeated me so completely, I could not but help see a link between the four-phased pattern in Master Dogen's works and The Four Noble Truths. Then, I started to think that possibly the biggest contradiction that Gautama Buddha must have faced in his thinking would have been between the subjective, idealistic thought of traditional Indian religion and the objective, materialist philosophies of the Six Great Non-Buddhist Masters who were popular in India at that time.

I thought that Gautama Buddha's solution to this contradiction was his discovery that we are in fact living in reality; not, as idealists tend to think, in the world of subjective ideas or idealistic dreams, nor as materialists tend to think, in a world of objective matter alone. Gautama Buddha established his own philosophy based on the fact that we live in the vivid world of momentary existence, in the real world itself, here and now, merging and transcending idea and matter, the subjective and objective as an unbroken whole, which is reality. We exist, we live, we act here and now. This is the perspective of a religion of action. He used a method that brought together the two fundamental philosophical viewpoints into a synthesized whole. And the philosophical system he constructed in this way is the Buddhist philosophical system.

But at the same time, he realized that philosophy is not reality; it is only a discussion of the nature of reality. To express this real world in mere words is impossible. He needed some further method by which people could experience directly what the nature of reality is, a method of real action and practice, pure being beyond words. That method is *Zazen*, a practice that was already traditional in India from ancient times. Gautama Buddha found that when we sit in this traditional posture in quietness, we can taste reality directly. So he recommended his disciples to practice *Zazen* every day.

Sekishin: But Roshi's method of explaining The Four Noble Truths is just your own hypothesis...

Gudo: Yes. Although I believe that the theory is accurate by my eyes, it is still but a hypothesis. However, some 50 years have passed since the time I first adopted such a way of viewing The Four Noble Truths as the foundation for my own understanding of the philosophy of Buddhism. During that period, I have come to feel keenly that the foregoing explanation constitutes a most important premise for understanding the philosophy of Buddhism, and further, that if we do not comprehend The Four Noble Truths theoretically in the manner described, Buddhist philosophy will be rather beyond our understanding.

Sekishin: That being so, can you give me an example of the combining and interweaving of four ways of thinking which Roshi feels are unique to Buddhism and necessary to understanding The Four Noble Truths?

Gudo: The logic and reasoning that combines and interweaves the four ways of thinking unique to Buddhism can be found in and throughout almost every chapter of the *Shobogenzo*. But perhaps one of the clearest examples is found at the beginning of the chapter known as the *Genjo Koan*, which is the first chapter in the early 75-chapter version of the *Shobogenzo*.

Sekishin: You mean the section which states, "*When all things and phenomena exist as Buddhist teachings?*"

Gudo: Yes. Here is a copy just here,. Please do me the favor of reading the full section out loud.

Sekishin: "*When all things and phenomena exist as Buddhist teachings, then there are delusion and realization, practice and experience, life and death, buddhas and ordinary people. When millions of things and phenomena are all separate from ourselves, there is no delusion and no enlightenment, no buddhas and no ordinary people, no life and no death. Buddhism is originally transcendent over abundance and scarcity, and so in reality there is life and death, there is delusion and realization, there are people and buddhas. Though all this may be true, flowers fall even if we love them, and weeds grow even if we hate them, and that is all.*"

Gudo: Yes. Thank you. What you have just read is the opening section of the *Genjo Koan*, the very first fascicle of the 75-chapter version of the *Shobogenzo*. Anyone who reads this passage will see, I believe, that this one section is divided into four parts. These are, namely, the part that begins "When all things and phenomena exist as Buddhist teachings," the part that begins "When millions of things and phenomena are all separate from ourselves," the part that begins "Buddhism is originally transcendent over abundance and scarcity," and the part that begins "Though all this may be true."

Sekishin: What is the meaning of the part that begins *"When all things and phenomena exist as Buddhist teachings?"*

MASTER EIHEI DOGEN

Gudo: "All things and phenomena" refers to the various forms and manifestations of that which truly exists, this real world we actually live and breathe in, or, to say it in other words, just this whole universe. Buddhist teachings are the teachings of Gautama

57

Buddha, the order of the universe as explained by Gautama Buddha. Accordingly, saying that all things and phenomena exist as Buddhist teachings means to attempt to see this very world of reality in which we are living from the standpoint of the teachings bestowed by Gautama Buddha. In fact, Guatama Buddha never taught that we should follow his teachings. What he taught is that we should follow and learn from reality itself. Still, when we attempt to think about this universe in which we exist in accordance with the meaning, values and other standards of judgment taught by Gautama Buddha, there will be the fact of delusion and of enlightenment, there will be practice, there will be the question of life and death, there will be countless Buddhas who have attained Truth, and no less there will be the multitudes of creatures who have not so attained. Namely, this is an apprehending of this universe in which we are living from a viewpoint of meaning and value and the ideal, grasping the universe from a position of comparison of the ordinary vs. an ideal; or, to simplify, it is the standpoint of idealism.

Sekishin: What you are saying is that, if we take the foregoing from the standpoint of The Four Noble Truths as found in early Buddhism, this is equivalent to the position of The Truth of Suffering.

Gudo: Yes, that is exactly right.

Sekishin: Then, what is the meaning of the next sentence, which begins, *"When millions of things and phenomena are all separate from ourselves?"*

Gudo: The meaning of "millions of things and phenomena" is about the same as the foregoing "all things and phenomena," and indicates this universe in which we are living. Accordingly, "When millions of things and phenomena are all separate from ourselves" means times when everything of this universe in which we are living is viewed without connection to self," or to say it another way, is viewed purely objectively without any connection to the subjective. Then in such case, there is no value distinction to be made between delusion and enlightenment, no division between Buddhas who have attained Truth and the multitudes of beings who have not. Further, even though we may speak of life and death, just because there is some physical and material change that occurs, there is no need to view that event as somehow special or of importance. Namely, in this sentence, we find the exact opposite of the idealistic viewpoint of the prior sentence, and encounter a clear statement of an objectivist, materialistic viewpoint.

Sekishin: So, it is the standpoint of The Truth of Accumulation or Aggregation as found in early Buddhism, namely, the perspective of materialistic philosophy.

Gudo: Yes. That is the only conclusion that I can draw.

Sekishin: And what of the section which begins, *"Buddhism is originally transcendent over abundance and scarcity?"*

Gudo: This passage is expounding a viewpoint of Buddhism that is neither a position of idealism, nor a position of materialism. The meaning of "transcendent over abundance and scarcity" means a vision of a world in which relativistic comparisons such as abundance versus scarcity, rich versus poor, and dualistic divisions such as that between the ideal and the material, can all be transcended, being thereby the Buddhist world. Therein, the question of life and death, the perspectives of delusion or enlightenment, the multitudes of those who have not attained Truth and the Buddhas who have, these all exist as undeniable, absolute facts and truth. Namely, here we are speaking of the world of action transcending thought, transcending the senses, the world of actuality.

Sekishin: And that is the standpoint of The Truth of Negation and Synthesis, The Truth of Self-Regulation, is it not?

Gudo: It is.

Sekishin: And this brings us to the sentence that begins, *"Though all this may be true..."*

Gudo: Just now, from the standpoint of The Truth of Self-Regulation, we expressed a denial of the vain attempt to think of the objective world using the head alone, or to grasp the universe by the senses alone, a denial both of idealistic philosophy and of materialistic philosophy. However, even this standpoint, even this level of The Truth of Self-Regulation—to the extent it is thought of as just another philosophy—even this is *not* the world of actuality *itself*. Therefore, putting aside the world of mere abstract philosophy, we must touch reality itself. And so, for such purpose, as a symbol for reality, for actuality *itself*, we have the flowers that fall despite our sadness, the weeds that grow thick though we wish it were not so. Namely, it is a world telling of a fourth place, that *reality*, actuality itself transcending and surpassing subjective and objective, is *just is what it is*.

Sekishin: And that is the standpoint of The Truth of the True Way.

Gudo: Yes. And the system called Buddhism or the Buddhist Way or the like, is a path that allows us to grasp this very same absolute reality, which cannot be accomplished by either a Western-style idealistic philosophy nor its opposite, a materialistic philosophy, nor even by mere words to merge and transcend both. Accordingly, as I have described, a fourth perspective, completely its own, comes upon the scene, and that fourth perspective was expounded by Gautama Buddha as the way that permits us, for the first time, to truly understand Buddhist philosophy by means of a progression, step-by-step, in accordance with the order and sequence of human thought. Thereby, this is the core meaning of The Four Noble Truths that we find in Early Buddhism.

Sekishin: So, to summarize, the system known as The Four Noble Truths constitutes not just one portion of the philosophy of Buddhism, but encompasses and contains within itself almost the entirety of that philosophy.

Gudo: Well said. And to the extent that this is not fully comprehended, Buddhism ultimately will never be understandable to us.

Sekishin: One more thing, if I may. You have many times used both the name Buddhism and the phrase The Buddhist Way, but what is the difference between the two?

Gudo: The word Buddhism means the teachings expounded by Gautama Buddha, and if we need describe Buddhism in a few words, anticipates a theoretical, philosophical content in its meaning. On the other hand, The Buddhist Way or The Way of the Buddha, also has the meaning of the teachings expounded by Gautama Buddha, and are simultaneously related to words such as ways of practical conduct, types of conduct bearing not just the meaning of some theory or teaching, but concurrently including and expressing within it actual practice, a putting into action beyond the merely theoretical; the world of Reality, the world of action.

V. A "WILL TO THE TRUTH" & RECEIVING THE PRECEPTS

STARTING ON THE ROAD OF BUDDHIST PRACTICE.

Sekishin: So far in our talk, Roshi, we have discussed how the centerpiece of Buddhist philosophy is an affirmation of the real world, that the concept of The Middle Way is intimately related to an affirmation of the real world, and that The Four Noble Truths, which, you say, can also be called The Theory of Four Philosophies, serve as a unique philosophical system of Buddhism supporting that affirmation. I'd like you to now explain what we should do specifically, and how we should act and live as Buddhists in light of all that.

Gudo: I do want to discuss this topic, for Buddhism is not some abstruse, abstract system far removed from real life. It is, instead, a religion of practical action and behavior closely tied to our ordinary, daily lives. So, it is very important to inquire into just what we should do, how we should act as Buddhists.

Knowing how to act, how to practice, is an especially important question and inquiry for people just starting off on the Buddhist path. The problem is, however, that this same inquiry is also a most difficult one for such people. The reason for the difficulty is that, when we first resolve to begin Buddhist practice or to study Buddhism, we have no idea as to exactly what kind of religion Buddhism is, nor what its teachings are with regard to some ultimate, undefined place or goal to which it is leading us. What is more, as we set out toward that mysterious destination which we do not understand, and as we move forward step-by-step in our actual practice toward some foggy objective, it is only natural that we be confused from the very outset as to the right course to follow, for we are practicing Buddhism in the dark.

Sekishin: That is just what I feel! But if that is the case, what should we do?

Gudo: Well, with regard to this situation, Master Dogen offered but one course of action to set us off in the right direction,

Sekishin: And what is that course?

Gudo: It is our personal establishing of a *Will to the Truth*.

Sekishin: What does establishing a "Will to the Truth" mean?

Gudo: The *truth* of "Will to the Truth" is written as *bodai* in Japanese. It's a word derived from the Sanskrit word *boddhi*, which has as its original meaning the actual, truth, or reality. Accordingly, establishing a Will to the Truth means our sincere wish to know the truth, to seek what is and is not the real. Since we have little understanding of Buddhism when we first set out in its practice, we do not understand how best to engage in its practice. However, Master Dogen, through his words in such works as the *Gakudoyojinshu* and *Shobogenzo*, has shown us that the arising within of a sincere wish to know what is real *is* the starting point, the setting out point for our Buddhist practice, and thus of the highest importance.

Sekishin: Can you explain this through a more concrete example?

Gudo: Well, take the example of a person who develops an interest in Buddhism and is first thinking of reading various books about Buddhism. In fact, people with such an interest are quite few and far between, relatively speaking. Most people, even if they have some interest in Buddhism, will put it off until they have some free time, which never comes, or end up being distracted by their other pursuits or interests. Or, they will hear from somebody that *Zazen* meditation is indispensable to the practice of Buddhism, but then, the number of people who will actually go out and find a teacher to instruct them in meditation are so few. Most people, in that situation as well, will put it off and put it off, or just forget about the idea altogether over time.

Sekishin: So, that means that an establishing of a Will to the Truth requires, more than anything, a practical, realistic way of living our daily lives, something practical we can actually do? What is needed, perhaps, is a means to keep the spirit of inquiry alive within us?

Gudo: Well, that is a way to say it in different words. In his *Gakudoyojinshu*, a text written to guide newcomers in the practice of Buddhism, Master Dogen stated that "the establishment of a Will to the Truth" is the same as just reflecting intuitively that our life must be instantaneous, fully here and now, without thoughts of the past or dreams of the future. Simply being present here and now, present in this very reality in this instant with nothing to search for, nothing to be sought, that is the *Will to the Truth*.

But at the same time, Master Dogen also stated that the arising in human beings, from various circumstances, of an earnest and sincere wish to know truth, to seek the real meaning of human life—a calling within that will not release one from that quest, as though to save one's own head from fire—such a conviction is *also* the actual state which is the establishment of a Will to the Truth. In such circumstances, when we concentrate our hearts upon the knowing of truth, upon knowing the real meaning of human life, the other problems that we usually think of as being *as important as life itself*—such as profit, fame and the like—become, instead, unimportant in its light. Master Dogen grasped that the state of our seeing into our being in the instantaneous present can also be the kindling of the spirit of inquiry, and is a state available to anyone, possible for anyone to attain, as both the starting point for our Buddhist practice, and an indispensable precondition for that Buddhist practice.

A "WILL TO THE TRUTH" AND RECEIVING THE PRECEPTS

Sekishin: I now understand how important to our early practice is an establishing within ourself of a Will to the Truth. Is there anything else we need take to heart early in our practice as Buddhists?

Gudo: Well, that would be something which is not to be separated at all from our establishing a Will to the Truth. In fact, it is really one and the same, an unbroken whole, constituting the formal aspect of establishing the Will to the Truth. It is, in fact, the first step in keeping the spirit of inquiry alive ... When a Buddhist seeks to commence upon the study of Buddhism, there is first a ceremony which should be undertaken: It is called *Jukai*, the Receipt of the Precepts.

Sekishin: What is the *Jukai* ceremony?

Gudo: *Jukai* is the ceremony in which one receives and undertakes the Precepts as a disciple of the Buddha.

Sekishin: That sounds, I think, like something to be undertaken solely by Buddhist monks ...

Gudo: No, not only so ... In *Jukai*, we find both the receipt of precepts intended for monks, male and female, and those precepts intended for all laypersons wishing to become Buddhists ... It has both aspects. Really, the precepts undertaken by monks and lay people in Japanese Zen are the same, and it is how the person receives them in their heart and life that is most important in determining their significance.

Sekishin: Usually, the ceremony in which someone becomes a Buddhist monk is called by us lay people as either *Tokudo* or *Jukai*. This is the first time that I have heard that there is a *Jukai* ceremony only for laypersons.

Gudo: Yes there is. Now, because Buddhism is in a rather low state here, the *Jukai* ceremony is very rarely held for laypersons in Japan. It has become more common in the West. However, in the *Shobogenzo*, Master Dogen specifically left us a chapter entitled *Jukai*, in which it is strongly emphasized that, when the Buddhist believer first sets out to commence Buddhist practice ... be it monk, be it lay person, no matter ... the initial needed steps are an establishing of a Will to the Truth and, hand-in-hand therewith, the holding of the ceremony of *Jukai*.

Sekishin: What exactly happens during the *Jukai* ceremony?

Gudo: Well, there are small variations in detail, but the heart of the ceremony is always the receipt of precepts from the teacher. The teacher reads the precepts, one following the other, asking after each, "Will you maintain this?" In response, the disciple intones, "I will maintain this well." That is the core of the ceremony.

Sekishin: What are the precepts which are the object of the ceremony?

Gudo: The precepts which are used in this *Jukai* ceremony are referred to, usually, as the *Sixteen Great Bodhisattva Precepts*, the *Mahayana Bodhisattva Precepts*.

JUKAI (RECEIVING THE PRECEPTS)

Sekishin: And what are those sixteen precepts?

Gudo: The sixteen precepts consist of the *Three Devotions*, the *Three Universal Precepts*, and the *Ten Fundamental Precepts*.

The Three Devotions

Sekishin: So, the first of the Sixteen Great Bodhisattva Precepts are known by the name the *Three Devotions*?

Gudo: Yes. These are the precepts of feeling devotion to the three highest treasures revered within Buddhism.

Sekishin: What does that mean ... the "three highest treasures revered within Buddhism?"

Gudo: These are the *Buddha, Dharma* and *Sangha* ... the three highest treasures to which we Buddhists should feel tremendous devotion, and therefore to be called the Three Devotions or Three Treasures. In Sanskrit, these three are referred to by the name 'ratna-traya,' which can be translated as well as the Three Jewels. I very much prefer all these terms to the often used Buddhist term The Three Refuges, for refuge strikes me as a concept that has been influenced by an idea of 'salvation' in Christian theology, for example, by an external savior. It is rather different.

NISHIJIMA ROSHI PERFORMING THE CEREMONY OF *JUKAI*

Here, the meaning of Buddha is most specifically the founder of Buddhism, Gautama Buddha, who is our first Buddhist ancestor. However, simultaneously, it means the many Buddhist ancestors who have merged fully into the teachings of Gautama Buddha, who have arrived at a state at one with Gautama Buddha. All are our Buddhist ancestors about whom we may feel tremendous devotion.

Sekishin: What, then, is *Dharma*? Does it express the same meaning we discussed earlier?

Gudo: Yes. *Dharma* means this very world of reality in which we actually are living, as well as the Buddha's teachings about the real world. Early in our conversation, I pointed out that Buddhism is a religion which reveres an affirmation of the real world. Dharma *is* this real world.

This world of reality, when looked at from an idealistic standpoint, is a world filled to the brim with events and situations that disappoint, which fail to satisfy or meet our expectations. And if we respond just by simplistically contrasting our ideals with the state of the real world, talking nonsense about how the world *should be* this way, or how things *would be* right *if only* they were that way - - Well, Gautama Buddha taught that human beings shall not find happiness by such a road.

On the other hand, we also have to keep in mind that Gautama Buddha did not mean that the real world is thus, in contrast, to be viewed but as a world of pure physical matter lacking all meaning and value ... something cold and dead and meaningless.

Perhaps this world of reality seems to us to be but a world of suffering filled with contradiction and irrationality and the like ... filled with many terrible things. However, there is another way to view this world, a Middle Way between those perspectives: even a world of suffering filled with contradiction and irrationality and the like, if we will but look upon it from a composed and still perspective ... observing calmly, watching serenely ... even such a place will manifest before us as a world of structured order, showing its aspect as an harmonious world in which contradictions and irrationality are swallowed up whole.

At bottom, this world of reality is the only world, the *alpha* and *omega* of a world, that we human beings possess. Thereby, if we but look well at this, our one and only - *alpha* and *omega* - world which we human beings possess ... awakening to the harmony contained within it ... employing that order as the standard by which to judge and regulate our conduct ... in the process, I dare say, making good contribution to the cultivation of an harmonious and peaceful society - - Such are, in Gautama Buddha's teachings, the duties that have been imposed upon us as human beings, as well as the way of happiness itself.

Thereupon, from such a perspective, Buddhism considers this world of reality ... this Dharma ... as among the highest treasures to which we human beings should feel deep devotion.

Sekishin: That brings us to *Sangha* ...

Gudo: The *Sangha* of devotion to the Sangha derives also from the Sanskrit language, and means the collective body of all Buddhists. Specifically, it points to the home leaving priests, both male and female, and the men and women who are home staying lay believers, together constituting the religious collective which is Buddhism.

No matter how noble and true the teachings of Gautama Buddha, if there were not Buddhist disciples to uphold the teachings and put them into actual practice, the teachings could have no worldly value. By such meaning, only when the home leaving priests and the home staying lay believers first did find the Buddha's teachings and sought to put them into practice as tenets of their daily lives ... only then could both the Buddha and the Dharma be said to have given rise to the value they each possess. From such perspective, Buddhism considers the community of Buddhists of the same high value to the Buddha himself as well as to the very order of the universe as expressed in the Dharma teachings of the Buddha. Of that same high regard is the body of all Buddhists who pursue, realize and bring to life the value to be found in both the Buddha and those principles which the Buddha teaches as Dharma.

The Three Universal Precepts

Sekishin: There is the next grouping among the Sixteen Great Bodhisattva Precepts ... What do the *Three Universal Precepts* entail?

Gudo: The Three Universal Precepts are the precept to Observe All Rules (Jap: *shōritsugikai*), the precept to Observe the Dharma (Jap: *shōzenhōkai*), and the precept to Work for the Rescue of All Living Beings (Jap: *nyōyakushujōkai*). Another way that these Precepts are expressed: *avoiding wrong, doing good, seeking to do good for others*. Both interpretations are common.

The precept asking us to *Observe All Rules* merely guides us to abide by, not only the Buddhist precepts, but all forms of rules and regulations of group life. Ordinary people, by the fact that we are people, do not live our lives fully independently and autonomously from each other, but are social animals who must gather together as groups of individuals in our lives. Thereby, when we are living and working together, person to person, various rules and restrictions will naturally arise to govern interaction within the group. This precept recognizes that our abiding by such rules and restrictions is an indispensable fact of life for Buddhist followers.

Sekishin: But Roshi, whenever there are rules … well, some laws and rules will be right and just, but some laws and rules will be wrong …

Gudo: Of course - that is true. I did not mean to say that all rules and restrictions will be just and proper. This precept of "Observe All Rules" is not asking us to follow blindly any rule or restriction simply because it is a rule or restriction. Instead, it is a precept expressing that we should generally respect the rules and restrictions which govern and naturally must arise when human beings gather in groups, in society. There is a tendency among some political thinkers to assert that all rules and laws are but methods for the strong in society to oppress the weak, and that anything which could be termed a rule or restriction, just by bearing such name, should be ignored, overthrown. Such thinking is, I believe, simply not right, is overly inclusive and heavy handed.

Sekishin: May we discuss the precept to *Observe the Dharma*?

Gudo: The real meaning of Observe the Dharma is to accept and incorporate within ourselves, to abide by the very order of the universe. It is the precept instructing us to study the order that is regulating this world of reality, just as we have discussed today

... Or to say it in other words, to study reality itself, as it is ... and to uphold and abide by the lessons derived therefrom.

Sekishin: What is its relationship to the precept Observe All Rules?

Gudo: Well, the meaning of Observe All Rules is to respect the rules and regulations which are existing around us, and Observe the Dharma means, in a larger sense, to seek to study the order at the very root of the universe, and to re-evaluate and guide our daily lives based upon the standards garnered thereby. Accordingly, we might say that the precept Observe the Dharma is more fundamental, more at the root, in comparison to Observe All Rules, and further, is providing us with supplemental details about how to live our life.

Sekishin: And what kind of precept is the precept to *Work for the Rescue of All Living Beings*?

Gudo: The meaning of Work for the Rescue of All Living Beings is to seek to bestow benefit upon all forms of living things ... not just to seek selfishly to benefit ourselves, but instead, to act by giving thought to all living creatures, great and small, existing beyond our own narrow selves.

By the way, many will prefer to express these Precepts along the lines of *"Avoiding wrong, doing good, seeking to do good for others"* and like expressions. Such interpretations are common too and may be used for bestowing the precepts. We will see that all the Bodhisattva Precepts really focus upon acting in helpful and good ways benefitting self and others, who are not separate, while avoiding harmful and hurtful actions toward self and others. Both interpretations guide us to work for the rescue and benefit of all sentient beings.

Sekishin: So, it is a most widely encompassing precept ...

Gudo: Yes. Among all the Three Devotions and the Three Universal Precepts, it is certainly a most encompassing and inclusive precept. The more detailed and specific a precept might be, the greater the likelihood that the precept will give rise to ill effects if it cannot be adapted to the different cultures, or to the norms of the different eras, in which it must be applied. Thereby, one of the wise points of *all* the *Mahayana Bodhisattva Precepts* is their flexibility and great inclusiveness.

Sekishin: You have mentioned the *Mahayana*, sometimes translated as "The Great Vehicle." This is part of the name, *Mahayana Bodhisattva Precepts*. What is the exact meaning?

Gudo: It means the "Great Vehicle," in contrast to the sometimes so-called *Hinayana* Buddhism, the "Small Vehicle." Actually, *Hinayana*, the "Small" or "Lessor Vehicle," is a critical name bestowed by followers of the so-called "Great Vehicle," contrasting their own beliefs to the tenets of other, earlier schools of Buddhism. However, "Small" or "Lessor" Vehicle really is not referring to the Buddhism of a particular place or era, but is something that anyone in any time might risk falling into. The difference these terms point to is really a matter of how to study and approach the Buddhist teachings. In undertaking the study of the very same Buddhist teachings, some persons might seek to grasp Buddhism through academic learning, mere reading of the scriptures or other forms of abstract discourse and debate ... this is called the Vehicle of Learning (sk: *shravaka*, Jap: *shomon*), and is the method of some schools of Buddhism as well as so-called "armchair" Buddhists. Another group of Buddhists emphasized what is called the Vehicle of Realization (sk: *pratyekabuddha*, Jap: *engaku*), a pursuit of Buddhism centered excessively upon stimulation of the senses with beauty, such as through viewing the natural environment, splendid temples, fancy rituals and costumes, the melodic chanting of *sutras*, the scent of rich incense, which can distract us with pageantry and aesthetic beauty alone. Some Buddhists may be too focused on their own personal peace, joy and saving while ignoring the welfare and suffering of *all* sentient beings. In contrast to such paths of The Small Vehicle, the way of the *Mahayana* Great Vehicle seeks to study Buddhism through pouring oneself, *losing* oneself through the concrete actions of our daily life, and to benefit all sentient beings. Studying Buddhist scriptures, academic study, viewing serene nature, chanting ... all are of great value. But, ultimately, the Truth of Buddhism is to be found right before us, in this real world, through our daily, most ordinary lives.

Sekishin: You are saying that the meaning of *"Bodhisattva"* in the *"Mahayana Bodhisattva Precepts"* refers to those people who seek to study and realize Buddhism though our real actions and conduct in ordinary life to benefit all beings?

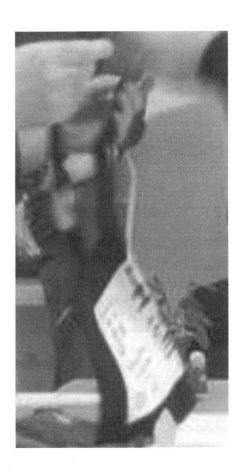

PRESENTING THE *RAKUSU* DURING JUKAI CEREMONY

Gudo: Yes, we can express it such way. That would be a characteristic of a *Bodhisattva*. As I said, the followers of the *Mahayana* teachings, The Great Vehicle which sets forth the way of the *Bodhisattva*, traditionally criticized the so-called Small Vehicle because, it was said, the *Hinayana* followers appeared to seek only their own enlightenment without thought of helping others ... The *Bodhisattva* ideal is one of *Compassion*, of self-sacrifice in the aid of the enlightenment of others. Buddhism teaches us that we are each and all part of the universe. We are not isolated elements, but facets of a grand whole, a whole that is reflected in every small part, in every being. So, if we are to express our true nature as human beings, it is natural for us to care for this which we have in common with all other beings in the universe. It is natural for us to work for the salvation of all living beings. Hand-in-hand with this, a *Bodhisattva* is a being who seeks to study and realize Buddhism through our real actions and conduct in this world, not in some world far removed. In this way too, followers of The Great Vehicle wished to stand in contrast.

Sekishin: You say that these precepts call upon us to study, and bring to life by acting in response to, the lessons learned in this real world. However, when I look at the Three Devotions and the Three Universal Precepts and the like which we have been discussing ... because the indicated proper conduct is so general and widely inclusive ... they seem not to spell out clearly just what precise, concrete behavior is called for in our real daily lives ...

Gudo: That is why the *Mahayana Bodhisattva Precepts* ... in addition to the Precepts of the Three Universal Precepts and Three Devotions ... set forth what are known as the *Ten Fundamental Precepts* ....

The Ten Fundamental Precepts

Sekishin: What is meant, then, by the *Ten Fundamental Precepts*?

Gudo: The Ten Fundamental Precepts are the precepts which charge us, as we can and acting sincerely, *Do not destroy life, Do not steal, Do not desire to excess, Do not tell a lie, Do not live by selling intoxicating liquors, Do not criticize the errors and faults of fellow Buddhists, Do not praise yourself or berate others, Do not begrudge the sharing of Buddhist teachings and other things, but give them freely, Do not yield to anger, and Do not abuse the Three Jewels.* Each offers to us more detailed, practical guidance on how we should act, how we should behave in day-to-day life.

Sekishin: At the top of the list ... What is the precept *Do not destroy life*? If that means Do not kill any living thing, it seems unrealistic to me, not possible. The reason is that, not only we human beings, but almost every animal must survive by sacrificing, by consuming other living creatures for food, whether plants or other animals. I think it the real situation that each living creature does what it needs to do to preserve its own life in that way. So, if we really try to follow faithfully this precept, the only way is by sacrificing our own lives ...

Gudo: Well, I think that what you are saying is quite correct..... Accordingly, this precept of *Do not destroy life* is not a precept forbidding the taking of all life whatsoever, but rather is a precept asking us to seek to avoid the taking of life

75

wastefully, without reason. This is the precept of our being mindful and reverential of all life, of our seeking not to be violent nor to kill as best we can. In this world of life and death, we should seek to preserve life where life can be preserved.

Sekishin: And the next precepts … ?

Gudo: *Do not steal* means to seek not to take without right or permission that which belongs to another. It is a respect for others by respect for that which may belong to others - not to take what is not given.

The precept *Do not desire to excess* is the precept of not giving way to lust and desire. The precept is sometimes stated as *Do not misuse sexuality*, specifically referring to carnal, sexual relationships, and asks us to be conscious and loving in our relationships, not greedy or driven primarily by physical desire, not trapped by excess desire or addiction, engaging in harmful or violent conduct, falsehood, abuse, harassment or the like. It too asks us to act with respect for others, no less for ourselves. I prefer to state it as *Do not desire to excess*, referring not only to sexual matters, but to all forms of desire, which should be kept in moderation.

Sekishin: I think that, traditionally, this precept was directed at monks both male and female who, having left their homes to take up residence in Buddhist monasteries, were often expected to avoid sexual conduct altogether. But, is it completely necessary to avoid everything sexual? How would this apply, for example, to Buddhists who are not residing in monasteries, who have home lives?

Gudo: Yes. Traditionally, there have been certain puritanical strains in Buddhism which sought to condemn all sexual feelings and contact, especially in the case of Buddhist monks, male and female, isolated in monasteries. There have always been some schools of Buddhism seeking to escape from the world, escape from the physical. But such is not the only way this precept has been viewed. In other interpretations, and especially for Buddhists with families and home lives, this precept has been understood traditionally as encouraging healthy relationships, that we should be conscious and loving in our relationships. For example, it directs us away from adultery, and encourages the wholesome, monogamous relationship of husband and wife. This is also a precept that is not seeking escape from the world and the physical, but rather, is guiding us to a nourishing life within it.

WITH *JISHA* TAIJUN SAITO, WELCOMING *JUKAI* RECIPIENT

Sekishin: What is the meaning of *Do not tell a lie*?

Gudo: We human beings, in our daily lives, tend sometimes to lie and mislead when it is expedient to do so, and we often do not feel very guilty about it. Yet, lying is the cause of the liar, himself or herself, developing a twisted and distorted sense of what is true … We sometimes lose our own discernment of honesty and truth and may, for example, more easily think it nothing to deceive others again and again. Further, the liar is the first to lose a sense of trust in life, is no less a victim of the lying. Thus, this precept asks us to honor honesty and truth, and is a most important precept to which Buddhist followers should pay heed.

Sekishin: Can you explain about the precept *Do not live by selling intoxicating liquors*? It seems very literal.

Gudo: Well, narrowly, it means not to take as one's profession the sale of alcohol. But, in its wider meaning, it might be said to mean *Do not abuse intoxicants*, and for us to exercise proper care of body and mind in such way. Ours is a path of moderation and of health and good balance in body and mind.

It should be remembered that our practice is founded upon the belief that all we need, all to be found, is to be found within this very mind and being as we are. Our path is *Zazen* meditation. Therefore, we do not encourage the use of substances such as alcohol, illegal drugs and the like to alter the brain for purposes of seeking what we seek … We need nothing more for our purposes than seated Zen meditation. In *Zazen*, we sit in the *real*, in the here and now. All we need is right before us.

Sekishin: And the next precept … *Do not criticize the errors and faults of monks and lay Buddhists… …*

Gudo: This is a precept pointing out that we should not be too critical or self-righteous when our Buddhist brothers and sisters, struggling as best they can to engage in Buddhist practice through the activities of their daily lives, stumble or fall off the path. In its wider meaning, it means to seek to avoid speaking of the faults of anyone in a way not helpful to that person, or in a way meant simply to praise oneself by comparison.

This leads to our next precept … *Do not praise yourself or berate others*. We should not praise ourselves, nor speak ill of others. We should be humble regarding ourselves, forgiving and not overly judgmental in our outlook toward other human beings. Although it seems a simple precept, I believe that it is one of the deepest in significance and import.

Sekishin: What is meant by *Do not begrudge the sharing of Buddhist teachings and other things, but give them freely*?

Gudo: It is the precept of not being covetous, greedy or possessive of anything, of the Dharma *which is* everything in this world. As well, Dharma also means the wisdom and knowledge taught by Gautama Buddha regarding the order of the universe. Thus, it refers to the treasure that is the teachings of the Buddha, as well as to all the treasures to be found in this world. Accordingly, *Do not begrudge the sharing of Buddhist teachings and other things, but give them freely* means not to overly distinguish in our minds between, nor to be possessive in our hearts about, that which is ours and that which belongs to others.

Sekishin: That leads us to *Do not yield to anger* …

Gudo: Yes. This precept reminds us that Buddhism asks us to maintain balance in both body and mind, and as one aspect thereof, guides that we should seek to avoid falling into extremes of emotion, be it sudden bouts of anger or of fear or the like ... We should seek for the calm and peace of the middle ground.

Sekishin: The tenth precept is *Do not abuse the Three Jewels*.

Gudo: And so we come full circle, back to where we began, at the Three Devotions. The Three Jewels means the Three Devotions of Buddha, Sangha and Dharma. The tenth precept is not to disparage or abuse, and to esteem each of these. If we fully wish to pursue the precept to esteem the Three Jewels, to revere the Three Devotions, this precept of not speaking falsely of the Three Jewels shows us a means to do so.

In conclusion, I believe that the rationale of the Ten Fundamental Precepts ... in fact, the rationale of all of the Buddhist Precepts, the *Mahayana Boddhisattva Precepts* ... is to serve as a guide, each pointing toward the best ways for us to live in this life, in this real world ... how to live benefiting both ourselves and others as best we can.

VI. KEEPING THE PRECEPTS & THE LAW OF CAUSE & EFFECT

KEEPING THE PRECEPTS: NOT SUCH AN EASY THING.

Sekishin: Roshi, you have just given me a very good, overall picture of the precepts … But, Roshi, do you mean to imply that Buddhism is a religion whose main concern is the strict keeping of the precepts?

Gudo: No, that is not what I wish to imply … As we see in texts such as the *Shobogenzo-Zuimonki* and in the *Shobogenzo* itself, Master Dogen often emphasized that having one's main objective as the overly strict keeping of the precepts is not really a beneficial attitude for followers of Buddhism.

Sekishin: So, if that's the case, what *is* the real meaning and significance of the precepts?

Gudo: The precepts found in Buddhism serve as criteria, as guidelines for the actions and conduct of Buddhists … Thus, it is not the case that all that need be done is the detailed keeping of the precepts, that if one keeps the precepts precisely nothing else matters. The real significance of the precepts is that they serve as the outer framework for our conduct, and within that frame the Buddhist must be able to freely act, freely choose and freely create the painting of one's own life.

No, the main goal of the Buddhist should not be simply the keeping of the precepts. Instead, we should know that if we move forward in the balancing and settling of body and mind through the practice of *Zazen* meditation, that if the center of our practice is *Zazen*, we will find that, naturally, we shall become *unable* to break the precepts even should we seek to do so! All we need do is to rely on *Zazen*, the true wellspring of our practice from which all else flows forth.

81

Sekishin: But, Roshi … I don't think that things can come so easily to the beginner …

Gudo: That is exactly right. However, if the beginner neglects the steady practice of *Zazen*, does not rely on *Zazen*, and simply has it in his or her head to focus on, to struggle doggedly to abide by the precepts … well, the result will never be good. The overly idealistic effort will be too much, will overwhelm one in the face of real life's necessities and limitations.

Sekishin: I suppose that such overly idealistic efforts of human beings will usually lead to failure …

Gudo: Yes. In his *Gakudo-yojin-shu*, Master Dogen stated, *"Even an ancient of great ability said the Buddha-Way is difficult to practice,"* by which Dogen expressed the reality that practice amid our day-to-day lives is not an easy course to pursue.

Sekishin: Well, if that is so for persons of great ability, then we ordinary people don't have a chance!

Gudo: Ha! But really, there is something to help us … Something does exist to help us as poor human beings who are always torn inside, perhaps never able to do just what we set our hearts on doing, simultaneously obliged to do many things we'd prefer never to do … There is something to aid us to mend the tear between our ideals, hopes and dreams and the hard reality, the ideal destroyer that the world can be … and that is *Zazen* meditation.

Sekishin: So, can it be said that *Zazen* is a very good medicine to help with this, to help us to be able to abide by the precepts?

Gudo. Yes, yes! That is the reason for *Zazen*'s role and importance within the way and principles of Buddhism.

But now, putting aside until later a deep discussion of *Zazen*, we need to touch upon the question of just why, to begin with, we find that we cannot maintain the precepts … …

THE LAW OF CAUSE & EFFECT

Sekishin: So, Roshi … just why do you think that it is so hard for us to keep to the precepts?

Gudo: To answer that, we need to think a little about the real nature of the precepts.

Sekishin: … And what is the real nature of the precepts?

Gudo: The real nature of the precepts is to express an aspiration and hope for the way human beings would *wish* things to be, would *wish* to behave … and a hope for how we would wish things not to be, what we would wish not to do. They are something born from a vision of the world and ideals formed within the human brain, our minds, and so if we were to say it in other, rather extreme words … they reflect an order born from the processes within our own human thinking, our thoughts and feelings … They arise from our own little heads.

Sekishin: Perhaps I do not understand. Are you saying that the precepts are not something objective, but really all are ultimately subjective in meaning?

Gudo: Well, I do not mean to say that the meaning of the precepts is but something which is completely subjective. There are many good, objective reasons for us to try to keep to the precepts, reasons based upon how best to live in the circumstances of the objective world. However, within the attitude to be found in people who are striving to keep the precepts, there is always included a most important subjective element. For example, some persons hold as an absolutist vision, as some hard iron rule, that they *must* keep the precepts … But from such a one-sided attitude, so stiff and inflexible, a freedom to act and choose in life shall not arise. Such a bound, imprisoned situation was called by Master Dogen *Butsubaku*, and *Houbaku*, which mean being all tied up in Buddhism, being wrapped up in the *Dharma*. It is our clutching onto the ideal that causes us to think we *must* keep, *must conquer* the precepts, and as a result to the extent that we get all wrapped up in seeking to attain the same … well, it means that

Buddhism, that the very order of this universe, will tie us up, will keep us knotted up in the strongest of imprisoning bindings.

Sekishin: How can we free ourselves from those bindings?

Gudo: To do that, we need to relegate to a shelf our basic vision of the precepts as inflexible moralistic standards, and instead, we need to look straight at, to view clearly, the objective world - the world of reality that surrounds and holds us.

Within our own heads, we rather wish that we were all knowing and all powerful, that we could do exactly whatever we may want to do, and not do whatever it would please us not to do. Yet, that is nothing but a dream world existing within our fantasies, and in actuality we find ourselves caught in a real world where no matter how much we were to wish it so in our subjective dreams, we cannot get things to be just as we would wish. One of the primary reasons that we find it sometimes so hard to stick to even the simplest of precepts is intimately connected to the fact that the real world we are living in will not accord consistently with the world of dreams, the artificial reality we create within our own little heads. Thereby, if we humbly study the realities of the objective world, what we discover as a solemn and undeniable truth, are the relationships of cause and effect, the *Law of Cause & Effect* ... That Law is both the source of our delusion and dissatisfaction in life, and by our coming to understand the workings of the Law, an aid in freeing us from that very delusion and dissatisfaction.

Sekishin: And those relationships of cause and effect, the *Law of Cause & Effect* ... is that connected somehow to the scientific concept of causation as, for example, we might learn in a science text?

Gudo: Yes, there is a very deep connection. When we study the natural sciences, in school for example, we are taught that all phenomena interrelate and are governed by cause and effect relationships. Thereby, the cause and effect relationships which control this real world thus control, not only the natural world, but no less our spiritual, psychological and social lives, a fact more and more understood as scientific knowledge has advanced.

Of course, science as we know it today had not yet developed during the age Gautama Buddha lived. Yet, despite that fact, through his great insight developed via long years of practice, and by his actual life experiences garnered over time, Gautama Buddha grasped that all that exists in this world is bound by cause and effect relationships. He taught this as the Law of Cause & Effect. So now, as the ages have passed, and as our means of expression have changed too, it is not incorrect to think of the Law of Cause & Effect taught by Gautama Buddha as being much the same as the laws of causation taught in our modern science.

THE TWELVE CAUSES

Sekishin: In what form did Gautama Buddha teach the *Law of Cause & Effect*?

Gudo: Whenever Gautama Buddha had the opportunity during his lifetime, he would explain this principle by stating that, for example, if there arises Cause A, thereupon Result A will occur. If there arises Cause B, thereupon Result B will occur. In this rather concrete manner, he explained the reality that all phenomena existing in this world interpenetrate and are governed by cause and effect relationships. Everything has its causes and its results.

Thereupon, as one set formula summarizing a group of such cause and effect relationships, the Buddha left to us what is known as the idea of the *Twelve Causes*, often called the *Twelve-Fold Chain of Cause & Effect*. In fact, we really do not know if the concepts of the Twelve Causes were actually the creation of Gautama Buddha himself, made during his lifetime, and the subject of their origin is subject to scholarly debate and awaits further research. But no matter … the Twelve Causes still serve as a cogent formulation explaining in easy to understand fashion a key aspect of the Law of Cause & Effect as taught by Buddha.

Sekishin: What specifically are the Twelve Causes?

Gudo: The Twelve Causes are (1) chaos (sk: *avida*), (2) action (*karma)*, (3) consciousness (*vijnana*), (4) the external world (*nama-rupa*), (5) the six sense organs (*shadayatana*), (6) contact (*spasha*), (7) sensation (*vedana*), (8) desire (*trishna*), (9) grasping (*upadana*), (10) possession (*bhava*), (11) birth (*jeti*), and (12) sickness, old age and death (*jana-marana*).

Sekishin: To begin at the beginning, what is the meaning of *chaos*, the first of the Twelve Causes?

Gudo: The first element in the chain of cause and effect is the most difficult to define. This *chaos* means the nameless chaos of a state we do not understand. We call it "chaos," for it is the ambiguous state which is reality, the source of all that is before the mind comes into play. At the beginning, nothing is clearly defined or distinguished from any other thing until the mind finds organization therein. In Enlightenment, such can be known as wholeness and balance, but in our ignorance such may seem as mere confusion and chaotic disarray. There is no figure or ground, no subject or object, no defined relationships of any kind, the whole merging into the whole. This first of the Twelve Causes is often referred to in Buddhist philosophy as primal *ignorance*, for such is very difficult to grasp or understand except by means of abstract concepts, and so in our ignorance, we do not know how to interpret the proper nature of things, we misapprehend this source of our existence, the conditions surrounding our birth. We feel enigma, complexity, division and an overriding sense of ambiguity with regard to the true state, wherefrom the notion of the person as an individual arises as something separate and apart from the real world, subject split from object, this from that. This process of division by mind into thinking, thinker and discriminated thoughts is the mental process being described in the chain of Twelve Causes, beginning with the following of the Twelve Causes which is *action*.

Sekishin: Are you saying that *ignorance* and *action* are not separate, but combine into a single thing?

Gudo: Yes. Action really can best be seen as something that combines action and chaos. Action arises co-dependently with the former. We might say that it is human action of the simplest kind, volitional but undirected action like the moving hands and feet of a newborn baby. It is much as the blind flailing about of the tiny baby who, still lacking clear sense of separate self, kicks and thrashes amid the chaos of the new environment where it finds itself. Thus, in the midst of the chaos, this movement or action naturally arises.

Sekishin: So, in Buddhism, this action truly sits at the start of all causal relationships?

Gudo: Yes. In the Judeo-Christian *Old Testament* there is the phrase, "*In the Beginning there was the Word.*" Or, if one is a physical materialist, one might say that force stands as the initiator. But if we speak from the standpoint of a follower of Buddhism, we must say that *action* is the beginning.

Sekishin: And how does this relate to *consciousness*, the next of the Twelve Causes?

Gudo: Consciousness, simple self-awareness, is a function of the workings of the brain, is possessed by each of us. Or, to say it in other words, it is the personal mind. It is one of the assertions of Buddhism that this mind, which each of us possesses, is formed and created out of the action that precedes it, a sense of self much as the newborn infant begins to develop a sense of self, a sense of separation from its environment as its arms and legs flail about amid the chaos, thereby coming to define space and dimension. And as the sense of *self* arises, the sense of *not-self*, of the external world, mentally arises as its reflection.

Sekishin: So, that leads us to the relationship of consciousness and the following of the Twelve Causes, the *external world*.

Gudo: Here, "external world" refers to each and every one of the individual things that exist, the multitude of phenomena upon which we have mentally bestowed names and identities. In other words, this is the objective world. It means whatever we can grasp with our senses, or if we were to say it in modern terms, it means the physical. However, the physical, the objective world, does not exist independently, but exists in a reactive, responsive relationship to consciousness, to mind, the subjective. It is the *not-self* reflective of *self*. This is the nature of the relationship between consciousness and the external world. The existence of mind, of consciousness, necessarily gives rise to the existence of ideas of an external world. But furthermore, the existence of the external world necessarily anticipates the existence of consciousness. A self entails a not-self, and not-self requires a self. So, there is a co-dependent arising, a relationship of interdependent existence, between consciousness and an external world. In Buddhism, this relationship of mutually dependent existence is often called co-dependent arising (Jap: *engi*).

Sekishin: And this connects to the *six sense organs*, the next of the Causes.

Gudo: The six sense organs means the six types of sense organ which receive external stimulation, and refers specifically to eye, ear, nose, tongue, body, and mind. In this list, body refers to the sense of touch, and mind refers to the center point of the other senses that integrates all components of the sensory system into a whole. It is through these senses that information on the external world flows into the brain to be further interpreted, details added to form our image of the world.

Sekishin: It seems like a very scientific way of thinking about things …

Gudo: It is. Buddhist philosophy was born out of the ideas of such earlier ways of thinking as Brahmanism and the Teachings of the Six Non-Buddhist Masters, and thus is a philosophy that arose as the product of an extremely thorough investigation and consideration of those earlier schools, their strong points and errors. For that reason, the theoretical structure of Buddhism is rather finely constructed.

Sekishin: That takes us to *contact*.

Gudo: "Contact" means the coming into contact of the six senses, the six types of sense organ, with the immediately prior of the Twelve Causes, namely, the external world which provides the external stimulations to the senses.

Sekishin: Which would bring us to *sensation*. What is meant by that?

Gudo: This is *sensation* as in feeling sensations. We might also call it *perception*. Just as *contact* is the passive form of one's coming into contact with the external stimulations, *sensation* is the active reception and taking in of external stimulations, the perception, the experiencing and actual tasting thereof in the contact.

Sekishin: Which then connects to *desire* in some way?

Gudo: Yes. We might also phrase this "desire" as "attachment." It is our attachment to the external sensations, which attachment and desire are born as a result of sensation. You see, because we now perceive *this* as opposed to *that*, such discrimination leads to likes and dislikes as we judge each seemingly separate thing, and the situation of wanting what we desire. This leads then to the next step, our efforts to reach out for what we want ...

Sekishin: *Grasping*?

Gudo: Yes. It is the conduct of *grasping* which occurs from the motive of wishing to acquire and make one's own, by hook or by crook, the things that are the objects of our attachment, our desire.

This brings us to *bhava*, the next link in the chain, which is the state of a sense of *possessing* which arises from that grasping. Such reaching out has a result: we do get something, and we develop a mental consciousness of possession and ownership. But this possession refers not only to a simple ownership of things as property, but to a fundamental sense of *having* something, for example, of having our own body and our very life. We feel that we have our thoughts and ideas, *our own* mind. Because such feelings of possession are fundamental to our sense of being, of having a life, it is sometimes called the *process of becoming* because it leads to the following link ...

EXCHANGE AT TIBETAN BUDDHIST CENTER

Sekishin: *Birth* ...

Gudo: Yes. This *birth* is life, our sense of being alive. It is our sense of our very lives, of our living which is born from the foundation of that possession. Thus, we feel that we were born. In other words, we feel that there is a *me* that we each possess, a separate body and mind, a self that is mine somehow separate from the not-myself rest of the world, and that this *me* is self-reflectively alive.

Sekishin: So, in Buddhism, it is thought that the state of possessing somehow gives birth to our life, gives rise to our mental sense of being alive?

Gudo: It sounds strange, does it not? In our common sense understanding, it may be hard for us to understand. But, such thinking places the fact of *possessing* in intimate relationship to life, our human lives. Such thinking is philosophically of very deep meaning I believe.

Sekishin: And so we come to *sickness, old age and death*.

90

Gudo: In life, as the years pass, we all come to sickness, old age and death. This body and mind we think of as our own to possess, and who we are and to which we cling, eventually grows sick and dies despite our desires otherwise. These are the solemn facts of life, which are to be found as the underside of birth and life itself.

Sekishin: So, the Twelve Causes come to a close with this final step of sickness, old age and death.

Gudo: It should not be understood in that way. It is not that the Twelve Causes draw to an end with sickness, old age and death, but rather all goes round and connects to the first link, to *ignorance and chaos*. In that way, our ideas of life and death, self and not-self and all the rest are swept up and merge, are wholly absorbed once we fully pierce that vale of ignorance. So, we really should view the Twelve Causes as constituting a circle, the last going right around to merge into the first. Thereby, it is often called by such names as the *Wheel of Causation*.

In this way, Buddhism holds, as one of its key foundations, a deep faith in the *Law of Cause & Effect*. If we only view Buddhism on a superficial level as a form of idealism, we may misinterpret, or completely overlook the significance of this Law of Cause & Effect. But we should recall that Master Dogen himself, in the *Shinjin-Inga* – the "*Deep Belief in Cause and Effect*"essay of the *Shobogenzo* – strongly asserts to us that a perspective doubting the Law of Cause & Effect is just not possible within Buddhism.

VII. THE INSTANTANEOUSNESS OF THE UNIVERSE

CONTRADICTIONS IN HUMAN FREEDOM

Sekishin: Earlier in our talks, I asked about our personal establishing of a *Will to the Truth* at the start of our pursuit of Buddhist practice. I recall that you said that this Will to the Truth is the state of mind of wishing to know reality, and that it is a very, very good thing when a man or woman comes to have such dedication, fully striving with all one's heart in that quest …. Did I understand correctly?

Gudo: Yes – That is just what we discussed.

Sekishin: But if I recall from our recent discussions, I think it was said by you that human beings are bound hard and fast, top to bottom, by the *Law of Cause & Effect*.

Gudo: Yes, that is right. The perspective of the Law of Cause & Effect is that our every action, without exception, has its origin in *a priori* causes stemming from our actions, as well as environmental and other factors that occurred in the past.

Sekishin: But if that is the case, I believe that there are some strange implications. For example, if we posit that we are firmly bound by Cause & Effect, by *a priori* causes and factors, then we human beings truly lack freedom of action, freedom of choice and free will. And if that is so, the discussion we had earlier on a Will to the Truth loses all real meaning … because we lack true will. On the other hand, if we human beings can establish within ourselves a Will to the Truth whereby we are filled with a passion to challenge and explore truth, and if that is to have some real meaning … then we must cast doubt on the idea that we are mere slaves controlled by some iron Law of Cause & Effect.

In any case, the idea of establishing a Will to the Truth must recognize the freedom of the individual, and the idea of the Law of Cause & Effect must deny the freedom of the individual. Accordingly, I think it most strange that the philosophy of Buddhism contains within it, side-by-side and intertwined, ideas both affirming and denying human free will.

Gudo: I see your dilemna. You have latched onto something very interesting, a seeming contradiction between Karmic causation and human freedom of choice and action.

Sekishin: Well then, Roshi, have you also noticed this contradiction between the two ideas?

Gudo: It goes without saying. In fact, unless we do take note of this contradiction between causation and freedom hich you have pointed out as existing within the philosophy of Buddhism, we really cannot understand correctly the philosophy of Buddhism at all. In fact, Gautama Buddha himself had a very precise awareness of this same contradiction, and the question of how best to resolve the contradiction was one of the issues of greatest import which he grappled with throughout his life.

Sekishin: Did he find a way to resolve the issue?

Gudo: Oh, yes! If Buddhism could not provide a clear means of solution, Buddhism would have failed in key aspects of its philosophy. But it did not fail, and thus has remained one of the crowning philosophies of the world, providing guidance of the greatest value to human beings over the millennia, no less now in the 21st Century.

Sekishin: What was the method to resolve the contradiction?

Gudo: That method of resolution was found in a vision of the *instantaneousness of the universe*.

THE INSTANTANEOUSNESS OF THE UNIVERSE.

Sekishin: The *instantaneousness of the universe*? What is that?

Gudo: If I were to describe in a very few words the meaning of the "instantaneousness of the universe," I would say this: Each and all of that which exists in this world in which we reside arises and takes place moment by moment, all while vanishing and passing away moment by moment.

Sekishin: That seems like a rather strange idea.

Gudo: Well, if we look at it from our ordinary, common sense viewpoints, it could be seen as strange. However, if we look at it from a Buddhist perspective, we see that the idea is straight on the mark as a statement of reality, and constitutes one of the pillars of Buddhist thought.

Sekishin: Might I trouble you to explain it in a way that may be easier to understand?

Gudo: Sekishin, when you think of time, into what categories do you consider that time can be broken down?

Sekishin: Well, that is difficult to say. But perhaps I would group time into, for example, past, present and future.

Gudo: Yes, yes. Past, present and future are representative categorizations of the concept of time. Now, tell me, Sekishin, do you think that we human beings can return, can travel backwards in time to experience again a moment that has already passed?

Sekishin: No, that kind of time travel is impossible, in both common sense and accepted scientific theory. For example, even if the most trivial matter, our actions of the past are past except in memory … No matter how much we might regret events or wish to make things otherwise, we can never reverse time and actually go back to the past to relive what has gone.

Gudo: And, likewise, do you believe that we human beings can access future times in advance, can experience a future which has not yet arrived?

Sekishin: No, that is also impossible. The future represents a time that has not yet come to be. Before it does come to be, we cannot live it or experience it except in our imagination. If that time were to come to be for us such that we were actually living it and experiencing it, then it would have become our present, no longer the future.

Gudo: Yes. We human beings can never go back into the past, can never attain the future before its time.

Sekishin: I think that is right.

Gudo: But on the other hand, we human beings can travel backward in our minds, in our thoughts and hazy memories, waxing nostalgic in our thinking about how things may or may not have been. As well, we can imagine the future in our dreams, with visions of how things might or might not turn out to be.

Sekishin: Certainly, we can travel back to the past in our memories, or look to the future in our dreams. But, of course, all that occurs in our heads. In reality, we cannot truly go back to relive the past, or travel into the future to reside there before it comes to be. That is just the hard reality of time.

Gudo: Yes. That is the reality of time. But, as we are not able to really live in the past now gone, and as we are not able to really live in a future yet to come, the one and only time we can live in is in this present. Yet, this present in time is continuously, moment by moment, simply the future becoming the present as the present turns into the past. Thereby, this time, which is the present, can never be anything except this continuous moment to moment.

If we think from a common sense view, we human beings feel, in some vague manner, that we are existing somewhere in an expanse of time, at a point on a time line, stretching from the past into the present connecting to the future. However, in our daily lives as human beings, if we try to think realistically about the situation, we are not living in some expanse of time stretching from the past into the present and connecting to the future. Instead, we must perceive that we are ever, always living just in this present, and nowhere else. We are living in the moment that is *this very* present that arises and passes away, in each smallest instant. And because this very time in which we are living is this moment, this very instant which is the present that arises and passes away moment by moment, when we hold up and reflect upon this world in light of such a vision of time, we must see that this world too, and all this world contains, arises and passes away, comes and vanishes moment by moment, instant by instant.

Sekishin: I see. This is something that we usually do not realize in our daily life, but when you state it in such manner, I see how we can view the world in that way.

Gudo: Certainly, it is not something that we become aware of easily in our day-to-day lives, but this instantaneous world that I have described *is* the world in which we are actually living. And this idea of the nature of the world constitutes the Buddhist concept of the instantaneousness of the universe, in Japanese … *setsuna-shoumetsu*. The word *setsuna* derives from the Sanskrit term *kshana,* an extremely small measure of time which we might refer to, in modern language, as an instant, a moment.

Sekishin: But how does this concept of the instantaneousness of the universe serve to settle the contradictions regarding human freedom presented by an idea such as establishing a Will to the Truth and the idea of the Law of Cause & Effect?

Gudo: With regard to that matter, Master Dogen, in the *Hotsu-Bodaishin* portion of the *Shobogenzo* for example, stated such ideas as, *"If all things did not arise and vanish instantaneously, bad done in the previous instant would not depart. If bad done in the previous instant had not yet departed, good of the next instant could not be realized in the present."* Namely, in this very world in which we live, precisely because it is arising and passing away, coming and going moment by moment … the good of the present moment can occur despite the bad which occurred in the moment before. The reason that it is possible for the good of the present moment to occur despite the bad which occurred in the moment before is just because this world is arising and passing away, coming and vanishing moment by moment, instant by instant. In other words, the events and circumstances of the moment before fade, thereby clearing space and time for the events of the current moment to happen … If circumstances did not change moment by moment, the world would be frozen and static. Thus, the freedom of action which we possess in the present moment can be sought in the fact that the time which is the present is an instantaneous existence.

Let us imagine that we are standing atop a place as thin and narrow as the blade edge of the sharpest razor. Just as we would then have the freedom to fall to the left or to fall to the right, the time of the present which is the stage for all our actions, the one and only foundation for our lives, is also a momentary existence of the thinnest and narrowest width, whereby, although we are bound within the world of reality, the world of actions, yet, we are free, and although we are free, we are nonetheless bound. We live on the razor's edge of the present, realizing the causes and factors of the past in this present, while realizing the content of the future through our present choices and acts.

Sekishin-san, have you ever heard, as one term representative of Buddhist thought, the phrase *shogyoumujou*, meaning the *impermanence*, the transitory nature of all worldly phenomena? It means that all our various actions are instantaneous existences, not possessing any lasting nature. Such thinking is the same as the idea of the *instantaneousness of the universe*, but viewed from its other side … meaning that our actions in the present, precisely because they are impermanent and transitory, are free yet fully bound by the past … and while fully bound by the past, yet are we free.

THE WORLD OF ACTION, THE WORLD OF REALITY.

Sekishin: I vaguely understand that, as you say, the concept of the instantaneousness of the universe expounded in Buddhism serves to harmonize the freedom denying perspective of the Law of Cause & Effect and the freedom affirming perspective of the Will to the Truth. Still, what you are saying is grasped by me only as a logical argument, and I really don't yet feel convinced about it in my heart.

Gudo: Yes. But if you could be completely convinced, to the very bottom of your heart, of the instantaneousness of the universe, a most important aspect of Buddhist philosophy would have become your own, would be in the palm of your hand. Still, that is not so easy to grasp right off, and I think it is to be expected that a complete understanding will take some effort.

Sekishin: If that is the case, might I trouble you to provide me with a bit more concrete discussion of the instantaneousness of the universe?

Gudo: Of course. I am happy to take our time to talk about time, and to approach it from various perspectives, until you can be convinced. Sekishin, you recall that early in our talks I spoke of the manner in which religions can be categorized into those religions venerating the *ideal*, those venerating the *material*, and religions of *action*.

99

Sekishin: I certainly recall that.

Gudo: In fact, this concept of the *instantaneousness of the universe* has a close, intimate relationship with the stated three categories of religion. If we hold to an idealistic standpoint, we can create various dreams in our mind's eye about how we might wish to now do this, or how in the future we should do that and make things become some certain way. However, what we must be aware of is that dreams are just dreams, and while beautiful in themselves, to make them have value in the world we must steadily, step-by-step, make use of the present moment and opportunity that has been granted to us. There is no other way but to move toward the dream step-by-step, instant by instant, in the present. If we should forget to make true effort in the moment which is the present, and if we should wish after the dream only as a fantasy within our own head, it will have no meaning for purposes of realization outside the mind, and we will end up coming face-to-face with the harsh reality of the real world, will be taught forcibly a cruel lesson in the fruitless pursuit.

In contrast, if we hold to a materialistic standpoint, we may view our present as merely the product of cause and effect relationships accumulating from the past, that the course of life's events is not dependent on our personal will, whereby we might think that there is no point in making any effort at all, best leaving all to fate. Thereupon, we might hold back on all idealistic efforts, and instead focus with greatest interest primarily on an analysis of the antecedent causes and their effects as the best way to understand how things necessarily will turn out. If we thus forsake the making of efforts in line with our will and desires, we then begin merely to drift along, entrusting our life and our fate to objective factors. Moreover, if we think of the meaning that should be present in one's being alive, living life, we are left to reflect on the meaninglessness we would then find in merely casting ourselves adrift to the unseen and impersonal forces of objective events and circumstances, having no regard to personal efforts pursuant to our personal will and desires.

However, should we come to awaken to the *instantaneousness of the universe* as put forward in the teachings of Buddhism, we awaken to the fact that the one and only time in which we can be alive is *this very present and immediate moment-to-moment, instant-to-instant*. Thus, Buddhism is a religion of *action*, for it focuses on our creating our life through our doing, our actions here and now. The reason we find in Buddhism teachings such as *"Life and Death are the Great Matter"* or, as found for example in the final line of the *Sandokai* of Master Sekito Kisen, *"Do not pass your time in vain"* and like instructions, is that the prime issue of human life is how to live life in this present instant, and that no other issue of human life is really possible … a viewpoint which results from a thorough understanding of the nature of reality.

To the extent that we understand the concept of the instantaneousness of the universe, we will know that there is no other way to live except in veneration of the real world, in veneration of the actions occurring in the present moment.

Sekishin: I wonder whether other concepts we have discussed, such as an affirming of the real world, the tenet of the *Middle Way*, the world of *action* and the like can be said to have been born out of the concept of the *instantaneousness of the universe*?

Gudo: Yes. It is a clear fact that the perspective of the instantaneousness of the universe pervades the whole structure of Buddhist philosophy.

VIII. HOW TO STUDY BUDDHISM

HOW TO STUDY BUDDHISM

Actual Practice

Sekishin: May I ask you to explain the method by which we might study Buddhism?

Gudo: I am happy to do so, because study is the doorway to the wisdom that Buddhism offers. However, first we must clarify what is meant by *study* in the Buddhist context. It is not only "study" in the usual meaning of that word. Sekishin, you recall that earlier in our talking together, we discussed how the first step in Buddhist practice should be the arousing, the establishing of a *Will to the Truth*?

Sekishin: I remember. We said that it's the arousing of a burning desire to know what is real.

Gudo: Exactly. However, even this arousing of a Will to the Truth requires, not just some mere thinking about Buddhism within the mind, but the commencement of a true exploration by means of actual practice.

Sekishin: What would be a specific example?

Gudo: At the beginning, a person who sets off to study Buddhism for the first time naturally cannot be expected either to understand exactly what Buddhism really is, nor whether Buddhism is or is not true in what it offers and teaches. Accordingly, the thing for that person to do is to actually test the waters for himself or herself via actual practice, to find out whether Buddhism is true or not in that person's life.

Sekishin: So, is the first step in the practice of Buddhism to doubt Buddhism itself … to doubt it, and initially to try it out before putting any trust in its teachings?

Gudo: That is right, that can be said. The typical religion will instruct that one should just believe, just have faith, with faith from the very outset being strongly pushed upon new followers or converts. But in the case of Buddhism, what is encouraged is a personal inquiry and exploration into whether Buddhism is or is not, in fact, a religion that merits belief. That is exactly the meaning of a *Will to the Truth*, an arousing of a burning desire to know what is and is not real.

Sekishin: So, we should believe in it –if and only if– it proves itself to be what it claims. And what means and methods exist to know whether Buddhism is or isn't true?

Gudo: For that, actual practice is required, actual experience. For example, while one might have previously known something about the Buddhist precepts, the important thing is just to see if one can abide by the precepts in one's own day-to-day living, in one's actual life. Perhaps something that is very difficult can only be truly felt and understood through real experience of that thing. Thereby, the actual practice of Buddhism is, in itself, just to grapple personally with questions of how difficult it is to uphold the precepts, why it is so difficult, and like questions. The important thing is to explore, experience and learn for oneself through actual doing.

How to Read Books on Buddhism.

Sekishin: Roshi, I understand that we should study Buddhism primarily through actual practice. Yet, some book study is necessary to introduce to us Buddhism's basic ideas and philosophy, is it not? Roshi, what is the best way for us to read and understand books about Buddhism?

Gudo: Of course, the reading of books about Buddhism cannot be neglected as one important aspect of Buddhist practice. However, even when we pursue the reading of such books, what is really most important is not the book, but the actual practice. If all we do is throw ourselves into reading countless Buddhist books just for the purpose of accumulating an intellectual understanding of Buddhism … well, the result is a thousand demerits and no merit at all. It is for this reason that the practice of Zen Buddhism has been called *a teaching beyond the scriptures*.

Sekishin: So, please give me concrete advice on the best techniques to read such books.

MASTER DOGEN

Gudo: Well, if I may speak from my own experience, I would begin by readings centered upon the writings of great teachers in the Buddhist world with whom one feels a certain affinity. In my case, I felt that early affinity to Master Dogen.

Sekishin: But the writings of Master Dogen are so incredibly difficult, and way beyond most of us as beginners, I think.

Gudo: Certainly - they are most difficult. But when one reads the works of a writer to whom one feels drawn, to whose personality one feels a great affinity, and if we read that teacher's words slowly, again and again, then little by little, the meaning will come to us. I believe that, more than reading the works of a variety of writers – a bit of this one, and a bit of that one – in the end, there is greater efficiency resulting from having centered one's early study upon a single teacher. The reason that I published my several books regarding the teachings of Master Dogen, such as my modern Japanese and English translations of the complete *Shobogenzo*, the book *To Meet the Real Dragon*, and others, was specifically for the benefit of those persons who might wish to study Buddhism via the teachings of Master Dogen, with the thinking on my part being that those books by me might be of some aid to such people in their pursuit. As I stated, Buddhist practice is really something apart from the mere accumulation of intellectual understanding and knowledge. For someone to select a great teacher in the Buddhist world with whom one feels a certain affinity, and to proceed to learn Buddhism via that teacher's character and ways, well, I think that to do so is both a practical way, and an enjoyable way to enter the gateway to the Buddhist teachings.

Sekishin: What do you think about reading *Sutras*?

Gudo: Do you mean the *chanting* of *Sutras*, the act of just *chanting* for chanting's sake, as opposed to really studying the message and meaning of the words they contain?

Sekishin: I had not thought about it.

Gudo: I do not place much weight upon chanting alone. Master Dogen said that we should read *Sutras* as a means to study what those books might teach on the subject of how best to engage in and realize Buddhist practice. Therefore, if we are to read the *Sutras*, we should do so by calmly and serenely reflecting upon and imbibing their meaning and content as we read them. Just to chant the words, perhaps in some ancient language one does not understand, singing the *sutras* mechanically for the singing itself, that is a way without real meaning I believe.

Sekishin: How can you say that? Isn't it true that, for example, monks are to be heard in monasteries and temples throughout the Buddhist world, morning and night, chanting *Sutras*?

Gudo: Well, even when monks may chant a *Sutra*, it is usually to be expected that they already have studied and grasped its meaning and content in depth beforehand. Anyway, these days, such chanting might be thought of as just training for their job as priests, training for when they might be requested to chant at funerals, memorial services and such from time to time. Beyond that, there is often only limited interest in the content. It is just what the priest is expected to do in their public, priestly role, a skill and performance the public expects of them. For me, what is important is not the chanting, but a thorough study and understanding and taking to heart of the valuable lessons the *Sutras* may teach.

Sekishin: A most prominent *Sutra* collection is the *Tripitaka*, the massive collection of *Sutras* and teachings and precepts first gathered and codified during the early centuries of Buddhism, and later added to with commentary and additional scriptures as Buddhism spread throughout Asia, to Tibet, China, Korea and Japan. Is it worth our effort to read all that?

Gudo: I would say that to seek to jump in and read through such a massive canon, and thereby to attempt to grasp just what Buddhism is ... well, I do not think it even possible. Just to read completely a single volume within the *Tripitaka* may require months or many years, and further, having read all of it would still not, I think, be equivalent to understanding truly the complete meaning of Buddhism. What is more, the various *Sutras* and other writings contained within the canon present so very many, radically different perspectives and ideas that it is nearly impossible to gather therefrom a single, unified vision of Buddhist thought.

Master Dogen referred to people who would seek to study Buddhism solely through the *Sutras* and the *Sastras*, the commentaries on the *Sutras*, and such writings as *Sutra* scholastics and commentary scholastics, and repeated again and again that such method cannot be expected to lead to a true and thorough understanding of Buddhism. It is an important point for caution in our seeking to study Buddhism. Much more is required for actual practice than reading and intellectual study alone.

Sekishin: So, Roshi ... How did you do your reading on Buddhism?

Gudo: In my case, I concentrated all my study efforts on single works by Master Dogen. When I was still a student in school, I happened to read a book called the *Shobogenzo-zuimonki*, a record of the words and stories of Master Dogen as written down by his disciple, Master Koun Ejo. It left me very, very moved at the attitude of total commitment on the part of Master Dogen in his own efforts to find truth. From that point, I sought to become fully familiar with other works by Master Dogen, such as the *Fukanzazengi*, the *Gakudo-yojinshu*, the *Shobogenzo, Eihei Shingi* and *Eihei Koroku*.

熊本・万日山時代 (47歳頃)

MASTER *HOMELESS* KODO SAWAKI

Sekishin: But those are all ancient texts written in 13th Century Japan, during the Kamakura Period of Medieval Japan, and I feel that, as such, they are so very distant in meaning and assumptions from us now … not very approachable or easy to grasp for the ordinary reader in modern times.

Gudo: Oh yes. Certainly, they are not so easy at the outset, and therefore it is also necessary to have an appropriate guide and teacher to help one work through them. In my case, I was fortunate to have received my original initiation into Buddhism through the kind and warm instruction of Master Kodo Sawaki, a teacher known by the nickname *Homeless Kodo* because of his habit of wandering here and there. Years after, I became a priest and received Transmission of the *Dharma* from Master Rempo Niwa, later the abbot of *Eihei-ji* temple, who instructed me in the traditional ways and forms of Buddhist practice.

I myself have instructed persons interested in Buddhism at long running weekly classes held at various locations in Japan, such as the Young Buddhists Association at Tokyo University and at the *Eihei-ji Betsu-in* temple, at our Dogen Sangha dormitory where visiting foreigners interested in Zen were able to live and practice under my guidance, at the Eastern Institute, on the NHK and other radio and television, and even for various large companies such as the Matsushita Electric Company at their Training Center in Osaka, and at other locations. Many of those classes were taught by me in English as well as Japanese, for students of Buddhism from all over the world whom, I thought, might find such instruction of use.

After many years of my teaching all these classes by myself, I have retired from several so to devote myself to writing and translation of Buddhist texts. Also, my health is not what it was, and I have needed to retire from many activities. Still, the classes in English and other languages continue under my Dharma Heirs in various places of the world, who also are working to pass on the true ways and forms of Buddhist practice. As well, over the years I have published a series of books in Japanese and English, such as my English translation with my student Chodo Cross of the complete *Shobogenzo*, the book *To Meet the Real Dragon*, and essays such as *How to Practice Zazen* and *Three Philosophies & One Reality*. Several of these have been translated into other languages such as Spanish, French, German and Hebrew. My purpose in writing each of these has been that, I hoped, they might be of some use as a good reference to persons who are newly setting out in their study of Buddhism.

A Basic Study of Philosophy

Sekishin: Besides the reading of books about Buddhism, is there any preparatory academic knowledge necessary or helpful for study of the Buddhist path?

Gudo: Yes, I would say so.

Sekishin: And that is?

Gudo: That is an understanding of the rudiments of Western philosophy, as well as a common sense understanding of the natural sciences, the humanities and social sciences, and sociology.

Sekishin: That's an opinion that I was not expecting to hear from you as a Zen teacher. I had thought that Buddhism portrayed itself as a religion transcending logic, and that a knowledge of general philosophy and science and such would not be of much use in its understanding. In fact, I would have thought that such forms of knowledge might even be harmful or counter-productive to an understanding of Buddhism.

Gudo: Well, I think that if you were to ask people about the traditional image of Buddhism, 8 or 9 out of 10 people would hold a view just as you expressed with regard to the relationship between Buddhism and philosophy and the relationship of Buddhism and science. But that is just a misperception among people who have failed to see the true nature of Buddhism. Of course, I do not mean to imply that, simply by studying science or philosophy, one will simultaneously and automatically thereby gain an understanding of Buddhism. However, because Buddhism is, in a certain meaning, an extremely logical philosophy, a very basic study of the concepts of Western philosophy … for example, Idealism and Materialism, concepts of self and of the objective world, of Man and God and Nature and such … may be helpful, and to have some understanding of those concepts makes an understanding of Buddhism that much easier. In fact, I believe that to someone lacking any familiarity with the basics of philosophy, Buddhism might even appear to be just nonsense and mumbo jumbo and virtually unintelligible in its elements. The reason is that the philosophical thinking

110

that existed in ancient India was much more advanced than many of us are aware, and for that reason, the specialized terminology to be used in any explication of Buddhism possesses a very high philosophical meaning and content behind it. Now, the philosophy of ancient India is not so familiar to many people, but Western philosophy is more widely known and accessible, and shares many parallels in subject matter with Indian thought. Accordingly, in order to understand such ancient philosophical systems and terminology in the present day, an effort to understand the relatively more accessible concepts of Western philosophy can be a great aid.

Sekishin: Well, doesn't that mean Buddhism is a religion which may be too difficult for the ordinary person to grasp?

Gudo: No. Not at all. Any person who has a real interest in his or her heart as to the meaning of human life, as to what is truly valuable in life, and other subjects of that type … such a person likely has already given such subjects deep thought, even if the person has never read some formal textbook on philosophy. So, I do not mean to say that a particularly deep and profound knowledge of formal philosophy is what is required. In fact, one must be careful not to get overly wrapped up and lost in intellectual ideas. Instead, what is required primarily is a relentless curiosity and questioning nature with regard to important questions such as the best path for one to lead one's life, one's purpose in life and how best to advance toward it, how one can find value and meaning in life and like matters. If a person is giving thought to such questions as a regular part of their daily life, that person naturally will be making a basic study of philosophy within their life, and will have philosophy as part of their life.

A Basic Study of the Natural Sciences

Sekishin: You also said that knowledge of the natural sciences is necessary to an understanding of Buddhism.

Gudo: We discussed sometime back that an important element of Buddhism is a belief in the Law of Cause & Effect. The study of the natural sciences is related to that fact, especially in these modern times. Even among people who have made a deep study of Buddhism, there are many individuals who still misunderstand the theory of causation found in Buddhism as some superstitious belief in a form of fatalism. That is a misunderstanding born out of an incomplete understanding of the true nature of Buddhism.

Sekishin: So, you are saying that knowledge of the natural sciences is necessary for a proper understanding of the theory of causation as espoused in Buddhism?

MASTER REMPO NIWA, 77th ABBOT OF EIHEIJI MONASTERY

TEACHER TO MASTER NISHIJIMA

Gudo: I am. There have been so many wonderful aspects to the development of the natural sciences in the modern era and present age. For example, at one time it was commonly believed that the planet earth is unmoving, with the sun, moon and other heavenly bodies circling around it. Of course, now we understand that it is our earth which orbits the sun. At one time, the evolutionary connections between humans and the other members of the animal kingdom were poorly understood. Now, we

112

understand that we human beings are but a species of animal ourselves, a creature evolved over countless eons from primitive organisms through mutation and competition for the fittest among life forms. Simultaneously, the workings of heredity and genetics have become so much better understood. Mankind has developed an understanding of the constitution of matter, and the field of atomic physics is making leaps and bounds in its comprehension of elementary particles and forces.

In this manner, the natural sciences have proven themselves time and time again in their ability to allow us to fathom the causal relationships governing the objective world in which we live and are part. Now, the fact that this objective world in which we live is bound up in strict relationships of cause and effect … that fact is now beyond doubt, as it is also beyond any doubt that the Law of Cause & Effect as taught by Guatama Buddha is an indispensable premise to a proper understanding of the workings of this world.

Sekishin: So, study of the natural sciences is useful to our comprehension of Buddhism.

Gudo: Yes. Of course, I do not mean to imply that an excessively specialized and detailed knowledge of many scientific fields is what is required. However, a grasp of the basic concepts of the law of cause & effect as adopted in the natural sciences is of extreme usefulness to an understanding of the Law of Cause & Effect in Buddhism.

A Basic Study of the Human & Social Sciences

Sekishin: And you say that a familiarity with the human and social sciences is useful to an understanding of Buddhism.

Gudo: Well, I do not think that the expertise of a specialist is required, yet a knowledge of, not only the natural sciences but also of the human and social sciences and sociology, can be important to understanding the workings of the Buddhist Law of Cause & Effect. For example, when we seek to grasp the true nature of the creature which is a human being, we tend - in our common sense understanding – to divide our human nature into a physical aspect and a mental aspect, the body and the mind, and we might take a position on which of the two is the most important to our being human. However, with remarkable advances in the field of psychology since the 19th century, the development of psychiatry, neurology and research on the workings of the brain, it has become clearer and clearer that the physical body and the mind are but two aspects of the same whole, that our tendency to think of each as a separate entity does not match reality. One centerpiece of Buddhist philosophy is the concept of The *Oneness of Body-and-Mind*, the *Oneness of Mind-and-Phenomena*, that the physical and the mental, the body and the mind are but two aspects of a single whole. Scientific study of the interrelationships of the human body and mind increasingly has shown the truth of this view of the oneness, the wholeness of the mental and the physical.

Most especially, beginning with Freud and the development of psychoanalysis in the 19th century, Mankind has reached into the world of the unconscious to clarify the inner workings of the mind. Such developments in psychoanalysis and other schools of psychology have been a great aid to our understanding of the descriptions of human psychology as traditionally stated in the old Buddhist *Sutras* and Commentaries. And also with regard to the unconscious mind, there is the whole subject of the *autonomic nervous system*, which can be thought of as a physical aspect thereof, and if I can briefly mention here something I hope to discuss later in our talk, the state of balance of the sympathetic and para-sympathetic nervous systems, two constituents of the autonomic nervous system in general opposition to each other. That state of balance is the true source of what we call in Buddhism by names such as *samadhi,* or equanimity, or the settled body and mind. All of this we have come to understand as the result of recent advances in the human sciences.

Sekishin: Can you say the same thing with regard to the social sciences?

Gudo: Yes. Human beings are, in their fundamental nature, social animals. Therefore, it is very important to make study of social phenomena and the causal relationships that arise within human groups. There are many areas of importance such as law, politics, economics, sociology, and to gather some understanding in each of those fields, and to study the mutual relationships which exist between Buddhist thought and societal phenomena, is very important from many perspectives. This includes in our considering the influence and effect which Buddhism shall have upon society in the future, as well as for pondering the possibilities for society overall to accept more and more and be open to Buddhism.

MASTER KODO SAWAKI IN *ZAZEN*

DAILY LIFE.

Washing the Face

Sekishin: If I may change the subject a bit … May I ask you to speak about how we might go about studying Buddhism in a non-bookish way, in how we live our ordinary, day-to-day lives? Could you discuss that topic?

Gudo: Ah ha, certainly. If you wish to study Buddhism, the Buddhist Way, in your daily life, it all begins when you arise in the morning. Washing the face, brushing one's teeth, such is the profound truth of Buddhism.

Sekishin: I would like you to explain that please. Everybody gets up in the morning, and everybody washes up and brushes their teeth. What can be so profound in that?

Gudo: It is often thought that the way of Buddha, the center point of Buddhist practice, consists of, for example, the chanting of ancient *Sutras*, bowing down before a Buddha statue, the burning of incense and the ringing of bells, etc., etc. However, each move of the hand, the way we take a step or pose the body in ordinary, daily life, all express directly, manifest fully, the Way of Buddha. Therefore, when we rise in the morning and wash our face, clean our teeth, this all springs from the balanced state of Buddhism, and are crucial to our Buddhist practice. In Master Dogen's *Shobogenzo*, there is a chapter simply entitled *Senmen*, Washing the Face. It offers a most detailed and scrupulous explication of just how Buddhist practitioners should carefully, sincerely undertake the washing of the face, should pour themselves into the very act of cleaning the teeth and the like. It describes such actions step-by-step, gesture-by-gesture, in minute facet. Of course, the outward forms of how such actions are performed will change with time, and from culture to culture, and it is not necessary perhaps that we mimic the exact patterns of movement and formality of gesture described in the *Shobogenzo*, directed at the lives of monks living in a mountain monastery of 13th Century Japan. But aside from the outward forms and formality, what is truly important is that, in the action, there is no separation between body and mind, and that, by relying upon just doing, we can live in the balanced state in the universe that is none other than truth itself. Thus, each act of washing the face, brushing the teeth, is a manifestation of the Buddhist Way, is an important Buddhist practice.

Taking of Meals

Sekishin: So, washing the face is an important Buddhist practice. What else is a Buddhist practice?

Gudo: Each and every act of daily life, without exception, can be Buddhist practice. But if I might speak of one particularly important act among all acts, I would consider the taking of our daily meals as deserving mention. Master Dogen has left us an essay entitled *Fushukuhanpo*, The Manner of Taking Meals, which minutely sets out the ritual, the detailed movements and gestures, of a monk in using the eating bowls and utensils traditional to monastic life. One line of that writing says, "*If there is equanimity in the taking of the meal, then all things in the universe are in equanimity. If all things in the universe are in equanimity, equanimity is the taking of the meal.*" The meaning here of the word *equanimity* is composure, stability, a maintained balance. People of a stable and composed attitude in taking their meals shall be of calm and composed attitude toward all the things in their life, toward all phenomena, the very order of the universe. And people who can meet all phenomena, the order of the universe, with stability and composure, can also attend to their meals with an attitude likewise stable and composed. That sentence expresses the meaning that Buddhist practitioners should be calm, composed and balanced in their repast as in all things.

Sekishin: I have heard that the meals taken in Buddhist monasteries are very rough and plain.

Gudo: Well, they certainly cannot be described as rich and opulent meals. However, because great care is paid in the labor of cooking, vigilance taken in the flavoring and seasoning, you would not receive the impression either that, in the reality of the monk's life, monastic meals are quite as rough and plain as you may imagine.

Sekishin: Even so, it is said, for example, that the rice gruel served for morning breakfast is watered down to such a degree, contains so little rice and so much water, that its surface can reflect the monastery ceiling like glass!

Gudo: Of course, there may have been those days when the number of monks in the monastery was very many, while the available rice was but little, such that the gruel had to be spread thin. On such days, one just makes do, accepts and is grateful for whatever is available. However, it would be a great mistake to think that it is a plus, or otherwise a good thing in Buddhist practice, to intentionally serve food of poor nutritional value, or to cause practitioners to tremble with hunger. Buddhist practitioners, no less for all persons, should seek to take food in moderate, yet fully proper and sufficient amount, and with healthful nutritional content and balance. Ours is a way of moderation, not wilful deprivation. But that being the case, when life does bring a person to those hard times when what is placed before the person is but a poor meal, or no meal at all, it is necessary to receive the same, to accept what is presented, without dissatisfaction, in equanimity and peace.

Sekishin: What about the eating of meat?

Gudo: I have heard it said that the monks of China do not eat meat at all, and are fully vegetarian. Even in Japan, it is the generally accepted thinking that it is best for Buddhist practitioners to avoid the eating of meat. However, I have some doubt myself about this prohibition on the eating of meat in Buddhism. This, again, is related to my belief that Buddhist practitioners, no less for all persons, should seek to take food in moderate, yet fully proper and sufficient amount, and with healthful nutritional content and balance. I believe that the body may require certain proteins and other nutrients that a purely vegetarian diet cannot provide. Further, I do not believe that the question is clear as to whether the Buddha himself believed in such a prohibition if one looks at stories of the life of Guatama Buddha. For example, there is the tale told of the Buddha's final meal, offered to him by one of his followers, a blacksmith named *Chundra*. From this, Guatama Buddha is said to have suffered a stomach ailment so severe, a terrible poisoning that led to the Buddha's death. Now, one theory holds that what *Chundra* served was a kind of mushroom. But there is also thinking that it was some kind of a meat dish. If that is the case, if the Buddha partook of such a dish, then it appears that there was no custom of not eating meat during the Buddha's lifetime, or else such a story would not exist about the Buddha having eaten meat before his death. The early Vinaya Code seems to allow the receipt by monks of donations of meat with certain specific restrictions. My understanding is that monks of South Asia still generally accept whatever is placed in their bowls by donors during alms round, including meat.

Sekishin: But one sees all through the *Sutras* and other Buddhist writings mention of a prohibition on eating meat.

Gudo: Oh, it is a fact that one finds such prohibitions all throughout Buddhist writings. But it is to be remembered that even the earliest *Sutras* were written well after the Buddha's lifetime, many hundreds years after that time. For that reason, it cannot be said that what is written in the *Sutras* always reflects the true thinking of Guatama Buddha himself, and this leads me to think that, perhaps, there might have been no blanket, unconditional prohibition on the eating of meat during the Buddha's actual lifetime. In fact, most of the strict prohibitions are found in later Mahayana writings and not in the earliest *Sutta*.

Sekishin: So, am I to understand that you accept the eating of meat?

Gudo: Yes. I have thought for a long time, based on my own personal experiences, that meat should not be prohibited to Buddhist practitioners. For me, it is all a question of moderation, harmony and of what is necessary for the health of the body.

Sekishin: Roshi, what do you mean by "based on my own personal experiences?"

Gudo: This is just one example of why I think some animal protein is necessary to the health of the body: When I was a twenty year old student, I used my winter vacation to stay at a monastery, and to live together with the young monks training there. During that time, an old woman, a devoted lay Buddhist, came to the monastery and donated, wrapped in newspaper, a great batch of dried sardines. Now at that time, meat of all kinds, fish too, was completely prohibited at that particular monastery, so the donation

119

gave rise to a big commotion and ruckus. I suppose they decided not to turn away the old woman, but the mere fact that there had been a donation of sardines caused, in a flash, all this whispering to start. And as each monk heard the news, one by one, some of them started, literally, to shake with joy. Within each of their heads, they were already tasting the flavor of something, a type of animal protein perhaps, that many of them had not encountered for years! Looking at their movements, well, they were jumping around with such craze and excitement, all in a way monks would not usually be seen to do.

FORMAL MEAL TAKING

Finally, as the time drew near for *yakuseki*, the evening meal in a monastery, and as the sardines were being baked in the cookhouse, the priests living quarters became filled with the smoke and strong scent of the fish. When they smelled it, the two cats living within the monastery premises became excited, and they began running and jumping around the room with such energy, that I thought they had gone completely mad. I noted that the young monks were not much better! It was such a pitiful scene! A bit later, when finally the evening meal began, all this serious chattering started among the young monks about the relative sizes of the servings of sardine to different people, that somebody's bit of sardine was bigger than so and sos and like talk. This led the senior monks to chastise the young monks, scolding with *"Do not lapse from the Buddhist Way in one's words"*, and like comments. When I saw all this, not only was I surprised at how serious and strict they were at the monastery about the prohibition on animal and other flesh, but I began to feel keenly that the prohibition on eating all meat might not be a plus for Buddhist practitioners, and might even be a minus in its effect which can cause such a loss of mental balance and stability through deprivation of needed nutrients.

Sekishin: I recall our previous talk regarding the precept *Do not destroy life*.

Gudo: Yes. As we discussed, the precept of *Do not destroy life* is not a precept forbidding the taking of all life whatsoever, but rather, is a precept asking us to seek to avoid the taking of life wastefully, without reason. This is the precept of our being mindful and reverential of all life, of our seeking not to be violent nor to kill as best we can. In this world of life and death, we should seek to preserve life where life can be preserved and to be humane. But, looking at nature, it seems that almost every living creature must survive by sacrificing, by consuming other living creatures for food. We cannot even take a step without killing some living creature under our very shoes, yet life will not allow us to keep always still. Of course, we should feel reverence for, and apologize to, those lives that are thereby lost.

Sekishin: So, Roshi, you think that the eating of all meat should not be prohibited.

Gudo: Again, for me, it is all a question of moderation, and of what is necessary for the health of the body. Of course, the other extreme is no better. If we are excessive in eating meat products, or any other food, the effect is not good for the body, and it can make us even hungrier and more aroused in appetite. Doctors say that excessive consumption of meat can result in a variety of physical ailments, to the heart and such, and this is to be avoided. On the other hand, in my understanding, a small amount of animal protein is necessary to both the growth of young people and to the maintenance of health among adults. I believe that allowing the same to be consumed for health reasons is, in fact, in keeping with the Buddha's teachings.

Sexual Desire

Sekishin: Besides the question of meat consumption, there is no less the question in Buddhism of marriage and family. What is your thinking on that topic?

Gudo: I think that it is perfectly natural for householders, persons living out in the world, to have wives, husbands and family. But I feel that it is advisable for monks in monasteries, male and female, to cut off physical, sexual relationships where they can.

Sekishin: Why is that?

Gudo: Well, it has been the custom in Buddhism since ancient times …

TRADITIONAL IMAGE OF THE TEMPTATION OF THE BUDDHA

122

Sekishin: So, it seems that some sinful aspect is being recognized in Buddhism in the physical, sexual relationships of men and women.

Gudo: No, that is not the case. Thinking both philosophically, as well as from my actual experiences and feelings in daily life, it is not correct to say that in Buddhism, in the manner of certain Western religions, a sinfulness or uncleanliness is being pointed to in the natural, sexual relationships of human beings. However, Buddhist monks, male and female, are specialists devoted to a search for Truth. Therefore, it was felt traditionally that in that search, the Buddhist monk should not be distracted therefrom by the great demands of romance and having a spouse, children and family. That has been the traditional custom for monastics. Of course, now we encounter that Japanese Buddhist clergy come out into the world after a time behind monastery walls, and so we must ask how to combine the roles of clergy and householder, as Buddhist priests who spend some time in life in the monastery, and then some further time in life to lead a *Sangha* or temple while also nurturing a family.

Sekishin: In the Buddhist world, there is found the concept of *issho-fubon*, which literally means "no transgression for a lifetime." It implies that not experiencing sexual relations at all for one's whole lifetime is an extremely commendable practice for Buddhists.

Gudo: Well, if that can be accomplished by someone, then I would offer very great tribute, as I think it would deserve both praise and applause. However, I think it gets priorities all wrong if a person neglects the true heart of Buddhist practice in order merely to attain some worldly praise and for having done so all one's life. According to the stories of the life of Buddha, even Guatama Buddha was married during his younger years, and was the father of a child named *Rahula*. Accordingly, I do not see need for us to desire to have a human personality even greater than that which the Buddha himself had.

Sekishin: Roshi, if I may ask a most personal question, I have heard that you are married, and have a wife and a family of your own …

Gudo: Please, always feel free to ask me about anything at all. There are no improper questions. Yes, I myself have a home and a wife. We have two daughters, one who was born to us and one we raised.

Sekishin: Yet, you were ordained as a Buddhist priest … ?

Gudo: Yes, I was ordained by my own teacher, Master Rempo Niwa.

Sekishin: So, how do you handle the circumstance of having a wife and family, while simultaneously being a Buddhist priest?

Gudo: I was ordained as a Buddhist priest, received *Shukke Tokudo*, on December 16, 1973. I retired from sexual activity from approximately 6 months prior to that time, from that May. I felt doing so would be right for me at that time.

Sekishin: Since you had a wife, how was it possible for you to do that?

Gudo: Well, until I really tried to do so, I myself doubted whether it was possible, and I did not have confidence that I could. However, when I really tried, I was able to get my family's understanding, and I was able to do it without too much difficulty. However, from the point of view of being a husband, it was something I pushed upon my wife for my own selfish reasons, and so I was always thinking that I had to compensate for it in other ways. Let me underline that it was a personal choice, and may not be appropriate for all Buddhist practitioners, whether lay or ordained. For some, having a spouse and family, having a home life, love and physical relationships … such paths may all be forms of Buddhist practice too.

Sekishin: Roshi, at that time, when you made that decision, you were already in your 50s. Do you think that it would have been possible to do such a thing as a younger man of 20 years of age, or in your 30s?

Gudo: Frankly, it would have been *absolutely* impossible for me. Let me spell that out clearly.

Sekishin: Is that because our sexual impulses are too strong when we are young?

Gudo: That is right. I do not wish to speak for all people, but the human sexual drives, when we are young, and as powerful as those drives are, are just not something that can be repressed easily by force of the ordinary human will. In addition, our possession of those drives is a most natural thing, and the fact that we have those sexual drives is the very reason that our human species still exists on this planet today.

Sekishin: So, what you are saying is that you do not deny our sexual side and drives?

Gudo: Yes, that is right. It is all a natural part of us. Because of the influence of Western religions, and their moral standards with puritanical aspect, we are apt in our current age to feel that some problem exists in our having those sexual drives, and to impose some feelings of sin and uncleanliness upon our sexual nature. There is also a puritanical streak in Buddhism, largely inherited from old Indian attitudes on the body and sexuality. But I think that to do so is in fundamental error.

On the other hand, I also do not agree with that portion of people who believe that sex, sexual pursuits, satisfying sexual urges and the like represent the highest happiness of human life, and that if only one could satisfy sexual needs, all one's problems in life would be solved thereby. Well, that is not the way either. The issue of our sexual desires is at the root of the human condition, a fact we human beings cannot escape or avoid. For that reason, if we are to handle and manage such a reality which goes to our most basic biological nature, what is necessary on our part is a great degree of care, discretion and balance.

Sekishin: I am just curious as to your views on sex education for young people ...

Gudo: Well, I certainly do not think that we should lie to young people. As well, it would be a disaster to teach some incorrect feeling of sinfulness or shame regarding the physical relationships of men and women, and adults should not respond to the innocent questions of children regarding sex by scolding them or deceiving them or telling them made up stories. When adults do such things, they merely multiply the problems that will occur later, as the child gets older. On the other hand, when a child is too young and immature to understand certain facts, I don't think it good to force facts upon the child ahead of his or her ability to understand, and a good deal of common sense must be employed.

Sekishin: What is your view on the promiscuous parties, the wild clubs and such which are popular with young people now, featuring a good deal of drug use and easy sex?

Gudo: I was born in 1919, which means that I am of a much, much different generation from today's young people. I have heard about the popularity of these types of events, and I certainly think there is nothing wrong with music and dancing and young people enjoying themselves. But, if the center point of the gathering is drugs and promiscuous sex, I think that such parties might constitute an assembly of people who have failed to understand how sex is something at the very heart of our nature as human beings, and that sex should be treated with a proper degree of seriousness and respect. Some of the people who gather at such parties may be hurting themselves, may be leading their lives in unnecessary disorder, and in some way will pay for their actions later in life. However, while they are intoxicated on drugs or alcohol, they won't much take notice of the fact that such injury will occur.

The Six Attainments

Sekishin: I think that our conversation has become very frank, and very interesting. But I would like to ask you if there are any other standards you can point to which show how Buddhists should lead their day-to-day lives.

Gudo: The so-called *Six Attainments* are standards for how Buddhists should lead their day-to-day lives.

Sekishin: Please tell me about the *Six Attainments*?

Gudo: The Six Attainments are generosity (Jap: *fuse*), endurance (*ninniku*), ethics (*jikai*), effort (*gonshojin*), balance in meditation (*zenjo*), and wisdom (*chie*), and are the standards for *Bodhisattvas* … namely, for people who are seeking to study Buddhism through their actions and conduct. They are standards such people should best keep in mind in their daily lives.

Sekishin: Why are they called *Attainments*?

Gudo: The name derives from the original Sanskrit word *paramita*, the meaning of which is, most commonly, to have reached the other shore, the course to be followed to reach the other shore, to reach the world of Truth. The *Six Attainments* are thus six courses, or methods of personal attainment, to arrive at the world of Truth.

Sekishin: Can you please explain the concept of *fuse*, or *generosity*?

Gudo: Generosity means finding the joy in giving. Master Dogen said that generosity is the state of not being avaricious, covetous or possessive.

Sekishin: I think, Roshi, that in today's tough, dog-eat-dog world, it is thought that if you just give your things away all the time, you will eventually end up starving!

Gudo: Yes. Certainly, the kind of thinking you just described is very much present throughout the world. However, we still need to think about whether or not that is really always the normal and ordinary state for human beings, and whether or not such manner of thinking actually brings or does not bring happiness to people.

Sekishin: Are you saying that the present tendency in society toward *Me-ism*, toward selfishness and focus upon one's own best interests alone … Are you saying that such a state is not the normal and ordinary state for human beings?

Gudo: Yes. Over my long lifetime, I have experienced several periods of history, each with its own ever-changing values and perspectives, and it leads me to think that the present self-centeredness that has become so common in society is not the best, nor a necessary way to think.

Sekishin: Why is that?

Gudo: Perhaps this is related to the observation that nothing lives in this world in isolation, all by itself. In Buddhism, ideas of the independent self are rejected as but shallow thinking, as are ideas that if one's own self is doing well, is in good shape, then it does not matter whether others are also doing well or not. In contrast, in

Buddhism, we are – *each one of us* – viewed as one molecule, one atom within the whole wide world, one expression of the whole wide world. Our self, and the narrow little world in which we think our self resides, consisting of such things as our family, our town, the groups and circles to which we think our self belongs, all these are not where we are truly living or to be found. Nor are we living in Japan, America or in another country, on the planet Earth, in the solar system, or in any other like place. In reality, we are but an element, a single facet of a jewel of unfathomable size and scope: this universe. We are nothing more than an entity that is a flash, a droplet of dew, a single and fragile bubble born within, and which is, the universe. I use the words "world" and "universe" here to mean *all reality*. Accordingly, even when we try to say such things as this is *me and mine*, or that is *not me and mine*, it is all really but a dream of little import, and I very much doubt that it is the kind of thing that is worth warring and fighting over as we often do in this world.

Sekishin: But, Roshi, does that kind of wild, cosmic talk have any practical meaning for us?

Gudo: Well, to the extent that you think that what I said isn't down to earth, you might be led to the kind of conclusion you just expressed. But there is, in fact, great practical meaning. Let's imagine for a moment two very ordinary, daily scenarios. First, imagine you are sitting on a crowded train or bus, and a frail old man of 60 or 70 years old is standing, without a seat, right before you. Now suppose you kindly give the gentleman your seat … and also suppose the opposite, that you pretend not to notice the man and just continue to sit yourself. In which scenario do you think you are more likely to feel a bit of happiness for what you have done? By which are you more likely to sense our deep interconnection? I do not mean to say that you need always give up your seat whenever you happen to be on a train or bus, whatever the situation. But, to the extent that, in a corner of your heart, the decision is reached to give up your seat, whereby you boldly stand up and do so, it is to be expected that you will taste via your action a feeling of richness and completion of a type not easily felt in this life. Granted, the foregoing is a very familiar and simple example out of our most ordinary daily lives, but it is no less Buddhist practice. It is Buddhist practice.

Sekishin: Please explain the next concept … *ninniku*, or *endurance*.

Gudo: The meaning of *endurance* is the focused, patient bearing of the painful and arduous, the difficult and the bitter. For example, because Buddhism offers one set of standards for leading our daily lives, it may be held in contempt, or even attacked and persecuted, by people who hold standards and belief systems that differ from Buddhism. We are sometimes seeing this happen, unfortunately, as Buddhism enters countries and cultures where it is not the dominant religion. One meaning of endurance is that such hostility may need to be endured patiently by Buddhists. But besides that, there will be all manner of times of pain and difficulty in any person's life when he or she must endure hardship. Also, there will be times of pain and difficulty in the pursuit of our Buddhist practice itself, which can be demanding. When one is in the midst of all such situations, endurance represents not a response flooded with emotion, with sorrow or fear or anger or other upset, but instead, a staid and peaceful patience, a calm and accepting persistent effort and striving in the face of whatever is presented before one. I always have felt that the secret for success in leading our human lives is to not be discouraged at times of misfortune. That is exactly what endurance is.

Sekishin: That is a nice explanation, thank you. Please tell me about the next of the Attainments ... *ethics*.

Gudo: The next of the Attainments, *jikai*, has the meaning of upholding the precepts. Earlier in our talks we discussed the various precepts: the *Three Devotions*, the *Three Universal Precepts*, and the *Ten Fundamental Precepts* which constitute the *Sixteen Great Bodhisattva Precepts*. The meaning is an observing of these precepts, not breaking them.

Sekishin: What is the next Attainment ... *gonshojin*?

Gudo: If I were to put the meaning in modern terms, it is *making effort, striving*. Buddhists seek to separate themselves from concerns for reputation and image, concerns about personal advantage and disadvantage, our own profit and loss and the like, all of which concerns are common among most people in the general society. Instead, Buddhists seek to lead their daily life in other ways, in accordance with certain grand principles, to live in accordance with our will to live as Buddhists while, at the same time, maintaining harmony with the other people in the world we know and encounter, harmony with the general society. To walk that line may require of one person the effort of a hundred persons. Thereby, the meaning of *gonshojin*, this effort and striving, is just our sincerity and diligence in holding to the standards for leading our lives taught in Buddhism, our ever and repeated striving through constant and quiet effort, step by tiny step to realize and maintain the same in our ordinary daily lives in this world.

Sekishin: That leads our discussion to *zenjo*, which you said is *balance in meditation*, I believe. Please tell me about that.

Gudo: The meaning of *zenjo* is the placing of our human body and mind in a good and balanced state, a condition of stable equilibrium. The *zen* of *zenjo* … and of *Zen* Buddhism … is a Japanese term derived from the Sanskrit word *Dhyana*, via its Chinese pronunciation *Channa* or *Chan* for short. Specifically, these words are all referring to *Zazen*, which means seated *Zen* meditation. The balance of the body and mind, the physical and mental state of stable equilibrium, obtained through *Zazen* practice is what is meant by *Zenjo*, the *jo* of which carries the meaning of balance and stability. I say body and mind, but in actuality they are a whole, so bodymind is not two separable things.

ENGLISH LECTURE AT THE TOKEI-IN TEMPLE

130

Sekishin: Are you saying that *zenjo* is pointing to what is primarily a physical and mental state, a balanced condition of the human bodymind?

Gudo: Yes. That is right. And the next, the sixth of the Six Attainments, is *chie*, or *wisdom*, which can be said to be pointing primarily to an intuition, a way of seeing, which comes from the attaining of balance in bodymind. I believe that it is closely related to a state of balance in the autonomic nervous system as distributed throughout the human body. When we realize some balance in our body and mental state, we realize through wisdom the balance that exists as all reality.

Sekishin: A balance in the *autonomic nervous system*. What do you mean?

Gudo: Yes. Medical research has now revealed the many ways in which practice has effect on the functioning of the human brain, on the human nervous system and throughout the human body. One of the effects of meditation that has become clear through medical research, and which I like to focus on, is the effect of meditation in balancing the human autonomic nervous system.

In addition to the more popularly known human nervous system, which allows us to experience sensations of, for example, hot, cold, pain, etc., there is another, no less important human nervous system running throughout most of the body, called by physiologists the "autonomic nervous system." In turn, this autonomic nervous system is further subdivided into two constituent systems, known as the *sympathetic* and the *parasympathetic* nervous systems. If I may generalize, the sympathetic nervous system is associated with physical excitement, whereby the heart, for example, is caused to beat rapidly and forcefully by its effect. Generally speaking, the sympathetic system brings about tensing, constricting and excitation of the body's organs. In contrast, the parasympathetic system has a relaxing effect on the heart, causing it to beat more slowly, although sometimes it may also serve to stimulate some parts of the body, such as the stomach and digestive system. The point is that the two systems are always working simultaneously and against each other, and serve to regulate a great variety of internal conditions within the body based on the relative strength and weakness between the two systems at a given time, according to which of the two is dominant at a given moment and their level of balance.

131

When the sympathetic and the parasympathetic nervous systems are placed in a state of balance to each other, are at equivalent strength, we are in a state of balance of body which will facilitate our obtaining a state of balance of mind, a state of relaxation and mental ease and equilibrium. On the other hand, if the two systems have fallen out of balance, we may be thrown into mental extremes of excitement, of an excess of happiness or an excess of feelings of sadness and darkness, and many physical complaints will manifest such as a variety of ailments of the stomach, an inability to sleep, an inability to relax related to stress, etc. Thereby, it is desirable for human beings to seek to attain balance in the autonomic nervous system as a form of healthful living. That is the meaning of *zenjo*.

Sekishin: Is it the same with *wisdom*, the sixth Attainment?

Gudo: Wisdom is what the body and mind manifest and realize when the physical body and mental consciousness are in a state of *zenjo*. As I said, when we realize balance in our body and mental state, we are better able to realize through wisdom the balance that exists as this whole universe, as all reality.

Sekishin: It is like 1 plus 1 makes 2 … right?

Gudo: Well, that is a nice way to put it, but the thing about such a mathematical example is that $1+1 = 2$ is a conclusion which is always the same for each and every person, no matter who thinks it, in any and all situations … $1+1$ is always 2. However, what is truly the most important aspect of decision making is the human ability to make judgments and life determinations at each instant, situation by situation, moment by moment in life. I believe that the aspect of human thinking which has one of the greater effects on whether a human being shall find happiness and contentment in life is the ability of that person to flow with and render judgments in life, situation by situation, moment by moment, which are right and proper to the changing situation. So, Zen Practice is about always meeting each changing situation, and is not a cut and dried formula. I believe that the state of the heart and mind which will, over a long period, lead one in the direction of human happiness and peace, and the ability to meet and render proper and right judgments amid life's ever-changing situations, allowing one to adapt to all changing circumstances like water flowing, is a state of balance in mind and balance in body. I believe that such state is the very meaning of *wisdom*.

The Four Methods of Human Relations

Sekishin: Thank you for your explanations of generosity, endurance, ethics, effort, balance in *Zazen*, and wisdom … the Six Attainments. Yet, when I look at any of those Six Attainments, I'm left with a feeling of there being such great depth of meaning that, well, it cannot be absorbed in a single bite. So, I guess I need to take some time to slowly digest and attempt each one. For now, however, please tell me if there are any other standards offered in Buddhist philosophy for the conduct of our daily lives?

Gudo: Another of the teachings, one that I would certainly be pleased if you would take to heart, is the teaching of the *Four Methods of Human Relations*.

Sekishin: That name does not ring a bell. Please tell me of these Four Methods.

Gudo: The Four Methods of Human Relations have been sometimes called the *Four Benevolent Ways of the Bodhisattva* … the *Shishobo* or, more formally, the *Bodaisatta-Shishobo* in Japanese. This is because they represent the path a *Bodhisattva* shall walk to arrive at Truth. In that way, they do resemble the Six Attainments, but if compared with the Six Attainments, the Four Benevolent Ways of the Bodhisattva can be seen as rather more specific and concrete, yet simultaneously a bit more inclusive and comprehensive. For this reason, the *Bodaisatta-Shishobo* can also be translated to mean The Four Elements of a *Boddhisattva's* Social Relations, or as I prefer, The Four Methods of Human Relations, for they spell out four ways for us to act and function within the social relations in which we find ourselves in the world.

Sekishin: Please explain each one.

Gudo: The 'Four Methods of Human Relations consist of generosity (Jap: *fuse*), kind speech (*aigo*), helpful conduct (*rigyo*), and identification and cooperation with other beings (*doji*).

133

Sekishin: Generosity, or *fuse*, is also one of the Six Attainments. Is it the same?

Gudo: Yes. Please think of them both as the same.

Sekishin: And what is *aigo*, kind speech or loving words?

Gudo: The meaning of *loving words* is simply gentle and mild speech, words of kindness, of peace. When a human being is in the state of *zenjo*, in the state of stable equilibrium in body and mind, and in a state of *chie*, in a state of Wisdom, the words which rise naturally from that person's lips are words of peace, gentleness, love and compassion. As well, if we approach the matter from the other direction, when people endeavor to speak in loving words, they will thereby facilitate the bodymind's attaining the state of stable equilibrium, and the resultant state of Wisdom.

Sekishin: Are you saying that, by trying to engage in gentle, loving speech in our daily lives, the world of Reality will thereby open to us?

Gudo: That is my meaning. And at the same time, we should think about the effect that our use of loving words will have upon the various human relationships with other people who surround us, the human ties in which we play a part. It is not so particularly rare that a person, perhaps beaten down by life and filled with darkness and grief, will see his or her life view changed simply because someone else was able to offer a few kind words of love and compassion. In the *Bodaisatta-Shishobo* portion of the *Shobogenzo*, Master Dogen stated, *"Kind speech has the power to turn around the heavens."* No less, such words can change people's lives, and perhaps the situation of the whole world. It is something that becomes so very obvious when we apply this practice in our daily lives.

Sekishin: Please explain *rigyo*, helpful conduct.

Gudo: *Helpful conduct* means to seek to make all effort for the benefit of other people. If we think that the first of the Four Methods, namely, *generosity*, holds the meaning of giving material things and mental value to others for their benefit, we find that *rigyo*, helpful conduct, means more of a giving of our actions and energies for the benefit of others. Now, when a human being is in the state of *zenjo*, in the state of stable equilibrium in bodymind, and in a resultant state of *chie*, in a state of Wisdom, the actions and conduct which arise naturally from that person will be this generosity and this helpful conduct. In this modern world, it is considered unavoidable, and even desirable, that people should work first for their own needs and self-interests, and that it is just to be expected that sometimes we will step on the needs and interests of others in the name of personal self-interest. Such is this dog-eat-dog world. It is the lack of tranquility, the loneliness and isolation prevalent in modern society that supports such ways of thinking, and we can also look at it all as something that need not always be present in society … for it is just a state that human beings have created among themselves, under special circumstances and for a certain expanse of history, through various erroneous preconceptions. It a state created by our thoughts, which exists only because our thinking makes it so. Change that thinking, change one's physical posture, change the state of the human mindbody to find balance and Wisdom, and it shall be possible to change the human world.

Sekishin: And that brings us to *doji,* which you stated is an *identification* and *cooperation* with other beings.

Gudo: Yes. *Doji* means to try to do the same as the other people in the world around us do.

Sekishin: I thought that Buddhism was teaching a path we should each walk alone, thereby realizing our own mind by our own self. I am a bit taken aback by a teaching that we should do the same as the other people in the world around us do. People are so different. It is impossible to agree and work harmoniously with everyone we meet.

Gudo: In Buddhism there is the teaching of taking a Middle Way with those who differ. Let me explain. If your thinking differs from the thinking of others around you, you should resolutely seek to pierce to the heart of your own thinking … because we Buddhist practitioners have a need to diverge from the thinking that is prevalent around us, and must pursue our own ways of thought and conduct. In many ways, Buddhist Teachings go against the grain of greed, anger and ignorant selfishness and the like found in much of general society. However, when the fortunate circumstance exists that we are able, simultaneously, to harmonize in some way with those surrounding us, we should strive to so harmonize and to pursue the same conduct as those around us. Because, in our daily practice as Buddhists, our purpose is not to violate norms or create friction with something or someone just for the sake of violation and friction itself, we are taught to try to harmonize our conduct to the extent that harmony is possible. Because we are living as Buddhists in the midst of the greater, surrounding society, this is a very helpful teaching. Further, even if our opinions might differ to a greater or lesser degree, in the midst of suppressing our own desires and opinions in life for the sake of overall harmony, we might thereby experience keenly and deeply the true feeling and meaning of living as Buddhists. There are times for us to be humble and self-effacing, not overly self-assertive and self-centered. That is good practice for us too.

IX. *ZAZEN*

TIED UP IN BUDDHISM, WRAPPED UP IN *DHARMA*

Sekishin: In our recent talks, Roshi, we touched upon the *instantaneousness of the universe*, as well as the fact that Buddhism is founded in the world of *action*, the world of our acting here and now, right now, in this instantaneous moment in which we are living. In that regard, I heard from you that Buddhism is intimately connected to our ordinary, day-to-day lives, just as they are and as we live them here and now. You spoke of the *Six Attainments* and the *Four Methods of Human Relations*, and of other teachings that all seem so simple ... simple at first, at least ... But, sometimes, I'm still left with a very strong feeling that these teachings are really quite difficult, if not impossible for someone like me to put into actual practice.

And in addition to seeming so difficult in theory and practice, Buddhism may appear to many people to be imposing a very strict morality, telling us that we must do this or must do that. I know that, as you explained earlier, the Buddhist precepts are much like guidelines for a healthful life, not matters of what we must do. Still, for the reasons I mentioned, as a religion Buddhism may sometimes seem to many people as if it's very cold and distant from ordinary life or that it is an abstract philosophy failing to offer a feeling of real help, with practical and workable solutions to our daily human problems.

Gudo: It's quite possible for people to feel such things. And both Guatama Buddha and Master Dogen noticed such possibilities and commented upon them. For example, you will find in the *Shobogenzo* that Master Dogen refers to something which he called *being tied up in Buddhism* and *wrapped up in the Dharma*. What he meant by those words is that, when we seek to study Buddhism and pursue Buddhist practice, we may run into obstructions and obstacles within our own little heads in the form of ideas of some Great Buddha or the like whom we must worship, or some *Dharmic* Law with iron commands and rigid rules we must obey and which bind us, whereby our ability to act freely will be lost in delusion and misunderstanding.

Sekishin: So, Roshi, if so, how then should we escape from being all tied up in Buddhism and wrapped up in the *Dharma*?

Gudo: As a means to free ourselves instantaneously from a state such as Master Dogen described, Guatama Buddha recommended something which, over the millennia, has become the heart, the axis of Buddhist practice, praised by countless great teachers since the Buddha's time: *Zazen*.

Sekishin: Was Guatama Buddha the first person to teach *Zazen*?

Gudo: If you mean was he the first to teach meditation, he was not the first. In ancient India, from many centuries predating the time of Guatama Buddha, there existed the practice of seated meditation performed – as in the *Zazen* which we engage in today – by crossing the legs, raising upright the back, linking the fingers much as we do. For that reason, when Shakyamuni first left his life as a prince, it is said that he initially sought instruction from such figures as *Alara Kalama* and *Uddaka Ramaputta*, great teachers of Indian religion who taught him to seek for Truth via practices much resembling *Zazen*, at least in outward form.

Sekishin: So, that means that Buddhism does not have a monopoly on *Zazen* as a method of practice.

Gudo: It has no such monopoly if one means as a form of seated meditation. Practices such as *Yoga*, an ancient practice that has now become quite popular in the West, also contain various forms of seated meditation much resembling *Zazen*. Of course, although the same in outward form, there are important differences.

Sekishin: So, what is the difference between *Zazen* and the meditation practices that existed in ancient India prior to the advent of Buddhism, or between Buddhism and other practices and religions such as *Yoga*?

Gudo: That subtle difference arises in the wondrous perspective I believe Guatama Buddha was able to make his own through the practice of *Zazen*. If I may refer to the three categories of religion I have brought up in our talks from time to time, the other religions and philosophies which existed in India prior to Buddhism, as well as Yoga and the like, might typically be categorized as religions venerating the ideal, each seeking Truth in some other, idealized reality, seeking for an escape from this ordinary world in which we human beings are living here and now. In contrast, Buddhism is a religion that places central importance upon our actions, practice and conduct in this very world and very moment in which we are truly living, here and now. Of course, escapist interpretations exist even within some interpretations of Buddhism, but in the Greater Teachings of Buddhism, the so-called *Mahayana* Teachings of the Buddha, life in this real world is brought to the fore. The true meaning of *Zazen* first becomes crystal clear when we revise our view of *Zazen* using this perspective of Buddhism, with its veneration of action, practice and conduct in this instant moment.

Sekishin: How is that?

Gudo: Because *Zazen* is one form of action and practice here and now. When we separate from the world of action and practice, and merely perceive things as abstract concepts or ideas, or when we only think about the external world from a standpoint of materialism as some other philosophies do, we cannot escape from being tied up in Buddhism, wrapped up in the *Dharma*. But by boldly and thoroughly devoting himself to the practice of *Zazen*, Guatama Buddha was able to grasp in clearest fashion a philosophy of *Zazen* as immediate and instantaneous rescue, here and now.

BUDDHISM & *ZAZEN*

Sekishin: If that is the case, can we then say that Buddhism is a doctrine born from the practice of *Zazen*.

Gudo: Yes. That is so. I mentioned how, after Shakyamuni took leave from his home, departing from his family's palace one late night, he first received instruction in seated meditation based in idealistic philosophies from Indian religious teachers such as *Alara*

Kalama and *Uddaka Ramaputta*. Later, while Shakyamuni undertook his long fasting and other ascetic practices of extreme denial, he also may have engaged in some form of seated meditation. It is not clear whether he practiced seated meditation during this period or not, but there are stories that indicate so, as well as pictures such as those of the emaciated Buddha in seated meditation. But when he later realized that asceticism is *not* the road to Truth, and thereupon engaged in his supreme practice at the foot of the bodhi tree on the banks of the Nairanjana River, the practice which he engaged in was *Zazen*. And it was that practice of *Zazen* which allowed him to make Truth his own.

Sekishin: And how about after he attained Truth?

Gudo: It is recorded with great frequency in the Buddhist scriptures that, no less after Guatama Buddha attained the Truth, whenever he would give a talk on the *Dharma*, he would enter into a state of balance in bodymind through *Zazen*, that he would commence his talks after first engaging in *Zazen*. Even after Guatama Buddha attained Truth, he continued to engage in *Zazen* as a standard part of his daily life. As he continued to expand and deepen the teachings of Buddhist philosophy, it is clear that he sought to prevent Buddhist philosophy from straying from its foundation in *Zazen* practice, the fountainhead from which it springs.

Sekishin: So, it might be said that without *Zazen*, the development of Buddhist philosophy would not have been possible.

Gudo: Yes. Because *Zazen* is the root and source of Buddhism, I cannot see how Buddhism would have been possible at all without *Zazen*. Kodo Sawaki Roshi, when he instructed me so many years ago in the practice of *Zazen*, would often recount the following classic lesson: to engage in *Zazen* is as to eat a sweet bun, while to read books on Buddhism, *Sutras* or the like is but to read descriptive words and writings about the taste of a sweet bun. Accordingly, to use only books on Buddhism and *Sutras* to explain the sweetness of Buddhism to a person who has never actually experienced *Zazen* is the same as trying to cause someone who has never tasted a sweet bun to savor that flavor through mere words and written descriptions alone. It is an extremely difficult undertaking, and quite likely impossible. That is a classic Zen teaching. The referenced example is most ordinary, but as one comes to experience, little by little, *Zazen* - and to understand its total meaning - the truth of what he describes is revealed.

MASTER NISHIJIMA *ZAZEN*

WHAT IS *ZAZEN* ?

Just Sitting

Sekishin: Well then, please tell me just what *Zazen* is in fact.

Gudo: First, *Zazen* is to place the bodymind into a state of erect and stable sitting. By sitting with legs crossed, bringing the hands together and raising upright the back, the skeletal frame of the entire body and the mind is placed into a sound posture. As well, all of the musculature of the body is placed into a stable and balanced state. The nerves

141

are placed into a stable and steady state. Balance is attained in the autonomic nervous system, which we discussed earlier in our talks, a neurological effect brought about through this practice. The endocrine system attains a normal range. This is all an aspect of the practice of *Zazen*. Master Dogen expressed this by the phrase *shoshin tanza*, meaning: *to correct the bodymind, and sit right.*

Sekishin: Is *Zazen* just a kind of physical training and bodily exercise?

Gudo: Yes, *Zazen* definitely has that aspect, but that is not all that it is. At the very beginning of our talks, we discussed the perspective in Buddhism known as the *Oneness of Body and Mind*, that the physical body and the mind are but two aspects of a single whole, and that for the human being, the physical and the mental are not separate existences, and so we speak of *bodymind*. Accordingly, in *Zazen*, a stable and sound state of the body helps bring about a stable and sound state of the mind, which is *Wisdom*, and instantaneously in Wisdom one encounters that all reality is balanced and nothing is lacking anywhere in the universe.

Sekishin: Does that mean that, if someone engages in *Zazen*, their feelings, their state of mind will be rendered *instantaneously* into a good, balanced state when they encounter *Wisdom*, and all reality will be tasted as good and balanced?

Gudo: Yes. The moment is complete. That instant is total realization with nothing lacking. When we engage in *Zazen*, from the first moment that we begin to do so, we are placed into a state of bodymind wherein we will know personally the great Jewel inherent in Buddhism. What is more, it is so even before we may consciously realize the fact! Master Dogen said of this: *"A beginner's pursuit of the Truth is just the whole body of the original state of experience."* The meaning here is that, when the beginner first tries *Zazen*, that itself is nothing other than the full and complete, authentic experience of all that is contained just there, just then, in that act. The very sitting of *Zazen* is, even for the beginner who may not think so, already total realization of Truth just in the perfect action of sitting.

Sekishin: But I think that *Zazen* is not usually thought of in that way by most people. I think the usual conception of *Zazen* is as a practice pursued over years and years by monks locked in monasteries, gradually deepening their practice so that one day they will undergo a great *Satori* experience or transformation.

Gudo: It is a fact that, in common perspective, *Zazen* is viewed much as you describe. However, Master Dogen did not understand *Zazen* in that way. In Master Dogen's view, *Zazen* is not something that serves for purposes of an outside goal or reason other than *Zazen* itself. *Zazen* is the perfect and complete objective of *Zazen*. It is written in the *Fukanzazengi*, "*This sitting in Zazen is not learning Zen concentration … It is practice-and-experience which perfectly realizes the state of Bodhi.*" This means that *Zazen* is not undertaken in pursuit of some goal of reaching or achieving a state. Instead, *Zazen* is, itself, nothing other than the practice and the experience which in and of itself embodies, perfectly masters and encompasses reality. It is all right here in each instant of *Zazen*. How unusual is it in life not to do something for some ulterior reason, and just for the reason of the doing itself, finding all completion and resolution in such alone!

Sekishin: So, I suppose that the one and only thing that is really necessary in studying Buddhism is *Zazen*, and that nothing else is needed.

Gudo: Yes, precisely so. Of course, we may study this and that book, listen to teachings by Masters and such in order to better understand the wonderful richness of Buddhist philosophy. But Master Dogen used the term *Shikantaza* … Just Sitting … with the meaning that it is fully and completely enough just to sit *Zazen*, total fullness and completeness. It may sound strange to say to people uninitiated in Buddhist views. It is a bit like saying that many things are necessary to support and further our lives, such as to eat, to breathe, to study and work, the other people in our life, but yet, the moment we sit down and commence to sit *Zazen*, life is complete in that moment.

.

A Return to Original Self

Sekishin: I understand that Master Dogen told us: *Just Sit*. But what use is there in that, really? It sounds rather pointless.

Gudo: Kodo Sawaki Roshi, when he was instructing me in *Zazen* many years ago, used to say that every time he was asked by some student, What benefit will come to me from doing *Zazen*, he would answer in a booming voice … *Nothing comes from it at all!!* Sawaki Roshi would admonish all of us against the attitude of viewing *Zazen* as a means to a goal other than *Zazen* itself. He wished to strongly emphasize the sacredness inherent just in *Zazen*, that *Zazen* should be done simply to be done, without ulterior objective or purpose at all.

Sekishin: But to tell us to do something that will come to nothing, that has no purpose. It has to sound like a great waste of time and energy!

MASTER KODO SAWAKI *ZAZEN*

144

Gudo: Yes. Sawaki Roshi used to boom, *Nothing comes from it at all!!* It was his way to touch and draw out in the people to whom he was speaking the spirit of sacredness inherent in *Zazen*. On the other hand, when I myself am asked what will come from doing *Zazen*, I like to answer … *Everything can come of it!!* I believe that this is also the case, just the same as Master Sawaki's words.

If I am asked, "Will *Zazen* serve as a means to calm my mind?" then I answer, *It certainly will!* "Will it restore my health?" I answer, *Absolutely!* "Will it make me a person who can get things done, who will be a great success? " *Yes!* I answer. "Will I become someone who is not fearful even in the face of terrible tragedy and looking death in the eye?" *You will become that person!* … and so on, and so on, I answer. In response to any such question, if the answer represents a change in a good and positive direction, then we can say that *Everything can come of Zazen!!*

Sekishin: But *come on!!* How can you claim that? Is there any panacea like that in this whole world?

Gudo: Yes there is, and that is *Zazen*. But please listen very closely to what I am saying: if we inquire into how we will each become through our *Zazen*, the answer is that we will, each of us, become but our Self, our True Self. A fundamental concept of Buddhism is that each human being, each of us, is a wonderful existence, lacking not one thing at all, not one thing in the least from the start.

Thus, "Will *Zazen* serve as a means to calm the mind?" Returning to our Original, True Nature, *what is there ultimately in need of calming? In the wholeness of this world, where is the friction between you if not separate from things as they are?*

"Will it restore one's health?" When one discovers one's Original Face, nothing in the least lacking …. *what need ever be restored? One's health is always precisely one's health.*

It is the same for each and everything desired. It is the same for being the person who can get things done, who is a success or one not fearful in the face of tragedy and death. For with not one thing to be added, nor one thing to be taken away, all that needs to be done is already done, all success right in hand just here and now, and there is never the slightest thing to fear.

This is the meaning of our reclaiming our True Self. Therefore, that which can be attained by one through *Zazen* is none other than our Original Face, That which you were before even your Mother and Father were born. It is called by such names and others.

Sekishin: I often hear the expression *jijuyo-zanmai*. Is that the same thing?

Gudo: Yes. *Jijuyo* means both to receive the Self and to use the Self. It combines both ideas. It means to come back to our Original Self, thereby to attain and reside in the free and unrestricted state. There is a chapter of the *Shobogenzo* entitled, *Jisho-zanmai*, or *Samadhi as Experience of the Self*. This also means our experiencing the state of our True Self, and is pointing to the same tone of meaning as *jijuyo-zanmai*.

Touching the Boundless World

Sekishin: I think that I understand a bit the idea that *Zazen* is a practice which returns us to our Original Self, but I am rather stuck on exactly what is this Original Self, on what our True Self is. Doesn't that idea contradict other Buddhist concepts such as Nothingness, or the perspective of No Self?

Gudo: First, among the many people who offer various explanations and teachings of the doctrines of Buddhism, there are quite a few who talk incessantly about *Mu* as *Nothingness* or the *Void*, which I feel is a great misunderstanding. Please do not do so. Even the translation *Emptiness* may mislead us by failing to convey the great *Wholeness* and *Fullness* of such. It is also short-sighted if realizing Emptiness alone is taken as the be all and end all of Buddhist doctrine. One can fall into extremes of understanding Emptiness in a one-sided way, a kind of Zen sickness. It must be doubted whether people who claim any of such views truly hold a right understanding of Buddhism. Of course, it is a fact that the doctrines of Emptiness and No Self (*Muga*) occupy a vital position within the philosophy of Buddhism. However, it is *not* true that Buddhist philosophy intones a nihilistic Nothingness, nor that it points to only extreme, one-sided views of Emptiness or No Self alone as the complete Truth of Reality. To believe so risks falling into extremes, which the Buddha repeatedly cautioned against.

Ideas such as Emptiness, No Self and the like can be thought of as stances or perspectives based upon the various standpoints of The Four Noble Truths, a topic we touched upon earlier. I mentioned that I have my own way of looking at the Noble Truths that I feel elucidates the traditional understanding. To begin, the world can be seen from an idealistic, subjective perspective I associate with the first level of The Four Noble Truths, which is The Truth of Suffering. By the The Truth of Suffering, namely, when we look out at the world through our eyes from a purely idealistic, subjective viewpoint, we can commit the error of unwittingly interpreting Emptiness or our True Self from a purely subjective perspective, as meaning that there is only our little self, our mind, the I and ego, whereby the whole world in which we are living is experienced totally from the perspective of one's self. This is to understand the world one-sidedly viewed from this idealistic, subjective stance.

Sekishin: If that is the case, what is the relationship to No Self?

Gudo: No Self, appraising the world from a purely objective viewpoint, means there is ultimately no I, no self-existence of mind, no ego. This is a perspective born in direct opposition to the subjectivist viewpoint, a perspective that the objective world of Emptiness is No Self. This is now a materialist stance. If we speak in terms of The Four Noble Truths, it comes from the concept immediately following upon The Truth of Suffering, namely, The Truth of Accumulation. In other words, when we now think from the objective, materialist perspective, which is directly counter to the perspective of The Truth of Suffering, we experience that all that truly exists is the objective world, the outside, material world, whereby the self, the mind, I and ego, are as illusions all just swept up and absorbed by the objective world, the outside, material world. This is No Self.

Sekishin: Then, how should we correctly think about the relationship between No Self and the concept of Return to Original Self we spoke about?

Gudo: *Zazen* is a form of concrete, real act. Therefore, to explain this in mere words is, from the very outset, most difficult, if not fundamentally impossible. This is why a noted monk of the 18th century, Master Shigetsu Ein, called it *Funogo*, the Inexpressible, that which cannot be expressed in words. The Chinese priest, Master Nangaku Ejo taught *"To describe the thing in words shall not hit the mark."* However, if we leave it at that, then both Buddhism and *Zazen* become impossible to explain using words at all. For that reason, as an attempt to explain and express these things in the closest way that might otherwise suffice, there were born the thousands of volumes, the tens of thousands of volumes of Buddhist scripture. Accordingly, an explanation of *Zazen* as a Return to our Original Self is nothing more than our attempting to express in words one facet of an act which, from the very first, cannot be expressed in words.

Sekishin: However, does our having an Original Self conflict with the perspective of No Self?

Gudo: From the perspective of the world we create by the thoughts within our head, namely, from the perspective of the world of logic, there may seem to be a conflict in the fact that our Original Self is somehow also No Self. However, *Zazen* is a form of concrete, real act, and is reality itself, whereby it is pregnant with any number of conflicting and contradictory elements and their resolution, just as is the state of reality itself. Reality itself is, through and through, an existence filled with conflicts and contradictions of every kind. Thereby, Buddhism can also be said to be a means to study and resolve that reality, so filled with conflict and contradiction, via the concrete action of *Zazen*.

Sekishin: So, *Returning to the Original Self* is one aspect of *Zazen*, and No Self is *also* one aspect of *Zazen*.

Gudo: Yes. That is right. All we are doing at this moment is looking at a single face of *Zazen*, seeking to grasp a limited aspect of something which, ultimately, cannot be so grasped, cannot be expressed in mere words.

Sekishin: Then, what is the No Self found in *Zazen*?

Gudo: From the very moment that we begin to perform *Zazen*, from that very instant, our bodymind realizes its original, proper state. For example, the autonomic nervous system and bodily systems are placed in balance whereby *Wisdom* manifests in mind, which is a return to our True Self, our Original Self, our true state of being. That is one reason Sawaki Roshi used to say that "*Zazen is the self, making itself into itself, by itself.*" As well, this process of our self becoming one and whole with our Original Self is for us to do away with the division of "subjective" and "objective", "self" and "other", sometimes so much so that we may even begin to lose conscious awareness of our small separate self. For example, scientific research on meditation has shown that, when the autonomic nervous system is placed in balance, its competing systems in stable harmony, there is no need for us to bring to mind our mental functioning nor to bring to mind our physical functioning, for all just function naturally without our paying them any heed. All drop from mind. This is the perspective from which Master Dogen wrote in the *Genjokoan* essay of the *Shobogenzo*, "*To learn Buddhism is to learn ourselves. To learn ourselves is to forget ourselves.*" This *to forget ourselves* is but the experience that, because of the balanced state of the autonomic nervous system, sometimes our body in consciousness seems to have vanished as an object of attention, and our mind in consciousness seems to have vanished as an object of attention. It can be so sometimes.

MASTER NISHIJIMA's FORMER DOJO NEAR TOKYO

But if I were to speak of the ordinary reality of *Zazen* in concrete terms, I would say that, by the practice of *Zazen*, we place ourselves into a state of stable and quiet sitting, wherein we can discover our True Self. And simultaneously therewith, we gain the ability to just view and observe as it is, *just as it is*, whatever phenomenon happens to wander into our field of vision. Specifically, we just observe the white wall we are facing in *Zazen*, and we just observe the spots of stain that may appear upon the wall, or the wooden panels and supporting posts of the *Zendo*. Whatever might come into our vision, we just observe *as they are* without judgment or pondering. When we just observe all without judgment, whatever comes, we have no choice but to see them all *as is*, not seeing more than what is there, nor less than what is there. To do so is to expand this very limited world in which we live into the boundless world that is reality. Habitually, we view ourselves as living within various narrow worlds constructed by human beings. We live in finite physical bodies and finite mental perspectives of the mind, all as individual members of our families, our schools, our businesses, our clubs, our nations and so on. We are under the illusion that such a narrow state is the sole and necessary state, the way things must be for human beings. However, as we sit with posture in upright and balanced form, simply looking upon the things which come before our eyes *as they are*, we forget all about the limiting worlds of categories human beings have constructed for themselves, which we are always, always constructing for ourselves within our heads.

Thereby, as we transcend and go past the narrow worlds human beings have created, we become aware through and through that we are living in a world of vast scope, a boundless world, the widest world. It is not the small world of our body or our mind, nor our family, nor the restricted world of our workplace or other organizations, nor the bordered world of our nation, nor even this whole planet Earth, nor confined by the far reaches of our solar system, or galaxies upon galaxies. Rather, by sitting with posture in correct and balanced form, simply looking upon the things which come before our eyes as they are, we move beyond each and every one of these spheres of limit, and experience that we are living right at the very heart of the universe, each as one aspect of this magnificent, boundless, wholeness of the universe. This is the very meaning of No Self. This is the very meaning of *to forget our self. Zazen* is the state of our experience of being a facet of a magnificent, boundless universe of scope beyond mere thought, seeing as they are the things that may come before our eyes. Accordingly, we may perceive the existence of some conflict and contradiction between Return to Original Self and No Self when we ponder those concepts in our mind, but through the actual practice of *Zazen*, each is unified into a single whole, and each is included harmoniously within *Zazen*.

If We Do Not Practice It, It Does Not Manifest

Sekishin: We just looked at *Zazen* from the perspectives of The Truth of Suffering and The Truth of Accumulation, in its relationship to the concepts of Original Self and No Self. Can we also look at *Zazen* from the vantage point of The Truth of Self-Regulation?

Gudo: Yes. Because *Zazen* is, at its most fundamental, one type of action, it can be said that *Zazen*, in its most fundamental form and essence, begins from the perspective of The Truth of Self-Regulation. Namely, it is the stage at which *Zazen* is done free of the intervention of theory. In contrast, the stage at which one might be sitting in one's library or armchair reading books on *Zazen*, that might be said to be completely unrelated to the true *Zazen*. Likewise, merely looking from a distance at someone else's practice of *Zazen*, perhaps to judge from afar that it looks easy, or looks hard or like wasting time, that too might be said to be completely unrelated to the true *Zazen*. The true *Zazen* becomes your own when you, yourself, bring your own body to bear, sitting down upon the *Zafu* cushion, crossing your own legs and linking your own arms, lifting up your own backbone and the back of your own neck, whereby the self is regulated as body and mind are brought into balance. Only then does *Zazen* first become your own. Book learning and mere observing of others as one might have done theretofore all produce but a phantom image of *Zazen* and are far distant from the real thing. Master Dogen said of this separation in the *Bendowa* chapter of the *Shobogenzo*, " ... *if we do not practice it, it does not manifest itself, and if we do not experience it, it cannot be realized*." In other words, only through the practice of *Zazen* can the true nature of *Zazen* be revealed. And only through the actual experiencing of *Zazen* can its true meaning be understood.

Sekishin: And this means to enter into the level of The Truth of Self-Regulation, which is also The Truth of Negation and Synthesis?

Gudo: Yes. The Truth of Self-Regulation is the stage of pure action. It can be called as well *The Truth of Negation and Synthesis*, for it is the stage that sweeps in and swallows whole both the ideal and the material, self and other, right here and now. As we have said earlier in our discussions, it is called the stage of action because it is realized now, is acting here and now and is our acting here and now. Thereupon, because this stage of action is, at this very moment, existentially the world of the instant moment, there is no room affording time to slowly contemplate this and that, nor room to confirm phenomena sensually ... Namely, the world of action is the world in which ideas and ideals are extinguished, and simultaneously, the world in which matter and the senses are extinguished. We sometimes use expressions such as *losing ourselves* in something or being *wholly absorbed* in something, being *swept up* in something to describe those cases in which we human beings are trying, with all our might and with our very lives, to accomplish some act or goal. This loss of our very selves is the stage of The Truth of Negation and Synthesis, and is the stage of true Emptiness. The concept of Emptiness exists in Buddhist philosophy representing the stage of The Truth of Negation and Synthesis that goes beyond and transcends both the idealistic Truth of Suffering and the materialistic Truth of Accumulation.

Sekishin: Is this the level of *munen-muso,* a state void of all ideas and thoughts?

Gudo: No, no ...We often hear people discuss *Zazen,* making reference to reaching some state of complete absence of all ideas and thinking, but that just comes from a great misunderstanding about *Zazen.* Because *Zazen,* as we discussed earlier, is one type of action, when we are engaging in *Zazen* and actually experiencing *Zazen,* we are fully conscious and aware of circumstances, and therefore some thought is present. Accordingly, our state when we are engaging in *Zazen* is different from, for example, a state of having lost consciousness, a coma or deep trance, or the state of death. Sometimes, I hear from students who are very worried about when, through *Zazen,* they will finally reach some stage in which all ideas are extinguished and all thinking has ceased, or some such state, but that is just an illusory state that various storytellers have invented and which many students have been fooled by, and all they are doing is worrying about a subject which is not fit for any worry.

Sekishin: Are you saying that it is fine to be thinking something during *Zazen*?

Gudo: That depends on what you mean. It would, of course, be erroneous to be intentionally thinking something during *Zazen*. For example, if you were so concerned about wasting your time that you spent your time during *Zazen* pondering the solution to some mathematical problem, personal problem or the like. Well, that would not be *Zazen*. You see, *Zazen* is not a complete absence of all ideas and thinking, but neither is it our chewing over, our clinging or paying attention to, the thoughts that might happen to drift into mind during *Zazen*.

Sekishin: What should we do when thoughts arise in the mind?

Gudo: When we observe that a thought has arisen … instantly just let it go …. just let it drift away, as if a cloud drifting out of view in a clear sky.

Sekishin: I am speaking from my small experience, but when I sit *Zazen*, I feel that thoughts spring up in my head even more!

Gudo: That is not because the *Zazen* is causing your thoughts to spring up. It is because our daily lives are filled with a constant sequence of thoughts and ideas that we cannot easily put to rest. Thus, when we engage in *Zazen* and are released from the constant chain of thoughts, the small handful of thoughts which may yet remain seem especially to stand out amid the surrounding clear. That is all it is, like a single, small cloud that is all the more noticeable in an otherwise cloudless sky. The fact that you are able to become conscious and aware of a single thought means that all else has become quiet and no longer draws your attention. So, we might say that becoming conscious and aware of such thoughts is, in itself, the effect of *Zazen*.

Sekishin: Do the thoughts stop coming after you have been doing *Zazen* for many years?

Gudo: That's not the case. First, the very nature of *Zazen* is not a matter in the least of awareness regarding whether thoughts are appearing or are not appearing. It is a matter of our root of *non*-awareness, of our own, original *non*-awareness. Non-awareness is not awareness, nor is non-awareness the absence of awareness, not *no awareness*, and not *awareness*. If I may speak physiologically, it is a matter of whether our physical state, of whether the autonomic nervous system and other systems of the body are in balance or out of balance. These systems function as physiological mechanisms controlled at levels not usually rising to the conscious mind. The state of the autonomic nervous system is closely related to the sub-conscious processes of the brain. Even should we wish to determine in our conscious mind whether the autonomic nervous system is currently in balance or not in balance, it is impossible for us to perceive it directly. For example, our stomach's functioning is greatly affected by the state of the autonomic nervous system, and its activities by the workings of that system. Even should we, for example, wish to intentionally halt our stomach's activities by our will alone, we most likely shall be unable to do so. However, through *Zazen*, we do have an ability to adjust such functions as our blood circulation, the workings of our internal organs, the release of hormones, sleep, all functions that are virtually impossible for human beings to manipulate through conscious will alone. Thus, while you are busy thinking that the central point of *Zazen* is whether thoughts are arising or not at the surface of the mind, you will be missing the real nature and effect of *Zazen*.

Sekishin: So, that means that the most important thing is just for us to do *Zazen*, without relation to whether thoughts arise or are not arising.

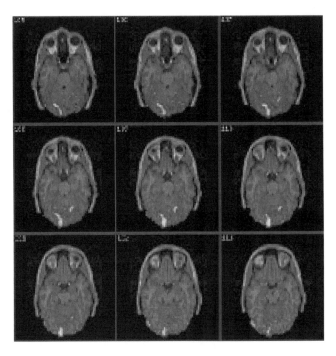

MASTER NISHIJIMA WAS A PIONEER SUPPORTER OF
MEDICAL RESEARCH ON THE EFFECTS OF *ZAZEN*

Gudo: That is exactly right. Just to be doing *Zazen* right this moment without relation to whether there are thoughts or no thoughts is, both from the physical aspect and the mental aspect, to be in the very same state as Guatama Buddha, right in this moment.

HOW TO SIT *ZAZEN*

Sekishin: So, Roshi, I am curious as to how you instruct beginners in the form of sitting *Zazen*. May I hear the specific instructions you give to someone doing *Zazen* for the first time?

Gudo: This is how I described *Zazen*, for example, in an earlier little book I wrote in English entitled, *How to Practice Zazen*. *Zazen* needs little space, just enough to sit with the legs crossed. To sit *Zazen*, select a quiet place in a room. We ordinarily sit upon a cushion called a *Zafu*. It is typically a firm, rounded pillow with a diameter of about 36 centimeters, which is a bit more than 14 inches. Traditionally, *Zafus* are filled with kapok, and depending on the body type of the person who will be using them, are in height somewhere between 10 and 20 centimeters, about 4 to 8 inches. The *Zafu* is packed tight with kapok so that it will keep a height of 4 or 5 inches (12 cm) when someone is sitting on it. The floors in most Western houses are hard, and so it is better to place the *Zafu* in a room that is well-carpeted, or place a mat under the *Zafu*. The Japanese-style mat, or *Zabuton*, is about 2 feet square and loosely packed with cotton or kapok to cushion the legs.

Sekishin: What should someone do if they don't have a *Zafu*?

Gudo: You can do many things, such as folding over a blanket to about the right height, making it firm to sit on. Cushions that are too soft, such as pillows, may not give the proper support.

Sekishin: How do we use the *Zafu*?

155

Gudo: Place the *Zabuton* mat and *Zafu* on the floor about 2½ feet (90 cm) away from a plain wall. Traditionally, we practice *Zazen* facing the wall, and there are two traditional sitting styles: The one easiest for most beginners is the half-lotus style, *Hanka-fuza*.

Sekishin: How do you describe *Hanka-fuza*, the half-lotus style?

Gudo: First, one should sit on the front half of the *Zafu*, with one's buttocks resting at the center of it, facing the wall. Then, bending one knee, bring the foot as close to the *Zafu* as you comfortably can, and turn the knee outwards so that its outer surface touches the mat. Next, put the foot of your other leg on the opposite thigh. It does not matter whether it is the right or the left foot on top.

HALF-LOTUS POSTURE

Sekishin: If I recall, in Master Dogen's instructions for *Zazen* written in the *Fukanzazengi*, he stated that the left foot is the top foot …

Gudo: That is correct. But, that was just for example. In my view, either leg on top is fine. If, during *Zazen*, one leg should fall asleep, it is acceptable to give a brief bow with hands pressed together in *Gassho,* and to discreetly switch leg position.

Sekishin: These sitting positions can sound painful to some.

Gudo: Yes, of course, it is rather difficult for beginners. So if it becomes too painful at first, one can change sides, placing the opposite foot on the thigh. As we practice regularly, our legs will become more flexible and the posture will become easier and more natural.

Sekishin: What is the full-lotus posture, or *Kekka-fusa*?

Gudo: The full lotus position is the standard, advanced posture for *Zazen*. First, place yourself into the half-lotus position. Then holding one foot in place on your thigh, grip the opposite foot with your hand and lift it up onto the opposite thigh. Thereby, your legs will be crossed with one foot on each thigh, and, hopefully, your knees will be resting on the mat. Such position will be uncomfortable and feel unnatural for most beginners, but with practice it will come to be quite comfortable. You will find it much easier to sit in the position after practicing the half-lotus' for some time to loosen up your legs and ankles.

FULL-LOTUS POSTURE

Sekishin: What about the hands?

Gudo: We use a hand position known as the *Hokkai-join*. With your legs in the half-lotus or full-lotus posture, place your hands in your lap. Place both hands facing up, with the fingers of the lower hand supporting the fingers of the upper hand. If your right foot is uppermost, then your left hand should sit atop the lower one, and *vice versa*. Curve your hands into an oval, so that your thumbs touch. Your thumbs should meet at approximately the height of your navel, and be resting lightly against your body. Hold your arms away from your sides a little, and allow your shoulders to relax.

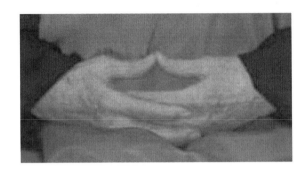

HOKKAI-JOIN

Sekishin: How do you position the head and neck? I have heard that you emphasize the position of the head and neck as being very, very important.

Gudo: Yes. Most important is to have the backbone vertical. If you look at Rodan's statue, *The Thinker*, the spine is curved and bent forward in that statue. We might say that such a posture represents the symbolic form of someone who is thinking about things. However, in *Zazen*, the objective is not to think about things, rather, what might be termed the objective is simply to taste the world of action here and now, whereby the back is to be held upright and vertical. When we perform physical labor, it is often asked whether or not we are putting our back into the work. Well, in *Zazen* too, we have to put our back into our *Zazen*.

Sekishin: How should we position the back?

Gudo: With your legs and arms positioned in the way I just described, stretch the back upwards gently. You might like to rock your head slightly from side to side, and front to back, until you can feel it sitting under its own weight on the top of the spinal column. Imagine that your spinal column is a column of bricks that you need to keep balanced vertically to prevent them from toppling over. The spine has a natural curvature, and we should aim to stretch the spine upwards in this balanced posture stretching just a little. To keep the back straight and balanced vertically is the most important point in practicing *Zazen*. People get into the habit of sitting with their backs

158

relaxed and rounded forward, but in *Zazen* we sit with the back upright. Holding the lower back straight sometimes takes some initial effort to overcome our daily habit, by pushing the buttocks out slightly and the stomach out forward. With the head balanced on the top of the spinal column, pull the chin down and back slightly, and stretch the neck lightly upwards as if being pulled up by a string attached to the crown of the head.

In this posture, sway gently from side to side until you find a position of balance in the middle. Your body should not be leaning to the left or right, backwards or forwards. At first, it is useful to ask a friend to check that your posture is correct. This straightness may not feel familiar or comfortable at first, since we rarely sit up straight. This straightness may first seem a little rigid, and it uses the body's natural balance to stay in position. One will become used to it soon.

To hold our spine naturally straight is the essence of *Zazen*. Keeping our spine straight allows us to enter a calm and balanced state of body-and-mind.

BALANCED POSTURE OF ZAZEN

Sekishin: What of the mouth and eyes?

159

Gudo: Close your mouth and your teeth. Breathe normally through your nose. Let your tongue sit naturally at the roof of the mouth, behind your teeth. Keep your eyes open naturally or close them halfway or a third. Focus your eyes on a spot on the wall about a yard or so in front of you, looking downwards at an angle of roughly 60 degrees; do not sit with your eyes unfocused.

Sekishin: Now that we have the posture, how do we begin *Zazen*?

Gudo: Sitting in the balanced posture as I have described, take in a deep breath and let it out. The tongue should rest on the palate. Then, sway the upper body two or three times to the right and left like a metronome, coming to rest in the center. Then begin the practice.

Traditionally, when we meet to practice *Zazen*, we walk up to face the *Zafu* and bow with joined hands to our own seat, and then turn clockwise to face outwards and bow to the other members in the room, before turning to the *Zafu* once again and taking up the posture. Then a bell is struck three times as a signal that *Zazen* is starting.

Sekishin: Some people prefer to sit in chairs, or in a position slightly varying from the half-lotus and full-lotus postures such as the Burmese, or to sit on a Seiza Bench, perhaps because of back or other physical issues.

Gudo: Well, if there is some necessity, for example, due to a medical problem, it is possible to sit stably in a chair or the like. However, the full-lotus posture and half-lotus posture are unparalleled in the stability they offer. Again, to keep the back naturally straight and balanced vertically is the most important point. That is my feeling on this issue, where I am rather a traditionalist.

Sekishin: What do you teach about breathing?

Gudo: Some sects of Buddhism teach that we should practice abdominal breathing or that we should deliberately count our breaths. Some also use *Koans*, or Buddhist stories or phrases to focus meditation upon. But these techniques are not part of *Shikantaza Zazen* practice. With the eyes open and the mouth closed naturally, we do not need to control our breathing, nor concentrate on thinking or feeling or a phrase. Sitting simply in the balanced posture is the beginning and end of *Zazen*. And it is this simple state, which we call experiencing reality, or experiencing the Truth, that Buddhist masters have used as the basis for their teachings. I believe so.

Sekishin: What is the meaning of the many puzzling, little Buddhist stories called *Koans*?

Gudo: *Koans* are stories used as a convenient means to allow us to penetrate the fundamental structure of Buddhist philosophy. But the true meaning and use of *Koans* has come to be wrongly interpreted over the years, I believe.

Sekishin: How so?

MASTER NISHIJIMA AT *SESSHIN* IN EUROPE

Gudo: *Koans* have come to be understood as conundrums the meaning of which should be penetrated *during* our practice of *Zazen*, as something to absorb the mind's focus *while* we are actually sitting. But this interpretation of *Koans* is completely different from their original use and meaning in Zen history. In the sitting of *Zazen*,

161

there should be no goal of something in need of being solved, no purpose or intent of wishing to solve it. Nor should our mind be focused on any object or point at all. In the true interpretation of Dogen's Zen Buddhism, *Zazen* can never be an intentional employment of devices making use of the mind, even if the ultimate objective is to transcend logic in some way. *Zazen* is just the act of placing the spine vertically, hands joined together and eyes cast downward, our breath in natural rhythm, judgments and other thoughts released. In that state, the body and mind are in balance just by themselves, and our *Zazen* requires nothing more.

Other people also misunderstand *Zazen* to be a kind of consideration or cerebral pondering, that we should think about miscellaneous philosophical problems intellectually during *Zazen*. Such an opinion on *Zazen* is completely wrong. *Zazen* is just our transcending both the intentional consideration of thought and the excited imbalances of body and mind, by means of our maintaining the stable, regular posture of *Zazen*. *Zazen* is a means for us to transcend the two fundamental intellectual philosophies of idealism and materialism by the act of just sitting, present in the moment as it is. It is our just being, whereby that perfect act of just sitting is the true manifestation of a philosophy of action. In that pure sitting, there is truly no other place to go or to be, nothing more to attain or to do.

Sekishin: However, in Western societies we usually translate the term *Zazen* as meditation, which is a word that means to think about things.

Gudo: That is true. But such an interpretation using Western terminology is just a misunderstanding of *Zazen*. The central criteria of *Zazen* can never be thinking about things, which is the central technique of Western philosophies that try to solve problems by use of the intellect. We too have a Buddhist philosophy to be understood through study, but that is not *Zazen*. *Zazen* is just transcending the intellectual area all at once and in this present instant.

Sekishin: Is it possible for us to do such a seemingly miraculous act?

Gudo: Yes, for it is just what Gautama Buddha taught us. He pointed to the doorway by which we might realize this True Being, this world of action here and now, summoning the capabilities present naturally within the human body and mind. By practicing *Zazen*, we can allow the autonomic nervous system and other bodily systems to be in balance. When this is done, we find our life as a true state of realization, as reality, right here in our sitting. In this way, we might say that the simple action of sitting *Zazen*, just by itself, swallows whole all reality, all time and space into that one place and moment.

Sekishin: I remember that Master Dogen wrote a book called the *Shinji Shobogenzo*, which is a collection of about 300 *Koans*. I believe you translated that book into English, did you not Roshi?

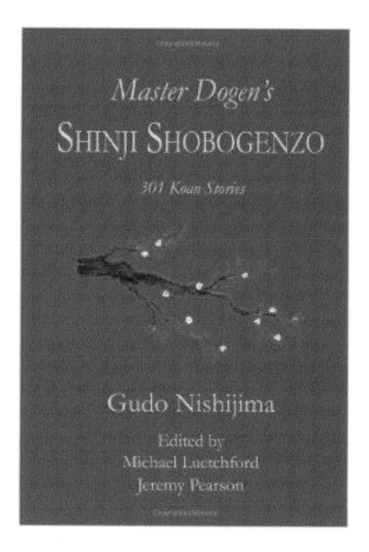

Gudo: Yes. But when Dogen compiled that group of *Koans*, he never used them for practicing *Zazen*. The reason he made such a book was just as an aid in the study of Buddhist philosophy.

Sekishin: Is it possible for us to understand Buddhist philosophy by reading that book? And is it useful for us to do so?

Gudo: It is. I think that Master Dogen collected many *Koans* for his own reference since the time he was young. *Koans* are very useful guides to the fundamental structure of Buddhist philosophy. His writings such as *Shobogenzo* are filled with references to traditional *Koans.*

Sekishin: What is the fundamental structure of Buddhist philosophy?

Gudo: That is just the four philosophies that we have been discussing in our chats from time to time, the fundamental structure of the philosophical basis of Buddhism. *Koans* were a creative, clever way invented by various Chinese teachers to summarize the tenets of Buddhist theory in a nutshell, as concrete, short stories that allowed the particular tenet concerned to be actually grasped beyond mere thinking about such things, to actually experience the tenet as fully present and real in one's life.

The structure of *Koans* are usually like this: first, a student and teacher might discuss a *Koan* only intellectually, for example, by the student expressing some understanding based on an idealistic viewpoint, or expressing something with a rather materialistic viewpoint, all on an intellectual level. However, to get to the real meaning of the *Koan*, the teacher must help the student to come to express the question of the *Koan* on a more realistic basis, as the Master suggests the real fact of experience, by guiding the student to the realistic viewpoint transcending the prior intellectual understandings, whether idealism or materialism. In this manner, the student truly pierces to the heart of the meaning of the *Koan*, and makes it his own, in his life here and now. From this viewpoint, I translated and annotated Master Dogen's *Shinji Shobogenzo* into English in cooperation with my long time students, Jeremy Pearson and Michael Luetchford. Thus, I think that *Koans* are very valuable to our understanding of the true meaning of Buddhist philosophy, but we should be most careful in utilizing them for their true meaning.

Sekishin: I see. May I not forget to ask how we finish *Zazen* when the bell rings?

Gudo: When the bell rings to finish *Zazen*, just remain quiet and calm for a moment. Do not be in a hurry to stand up. If your legs have gone to sleep, move them around until the feeling returns, and then stand up slowly. Traditionally, the bell is struck once when *Zazen* ends. After standing up, we straighten our clothing and, facing the *Zafu*, bow once with joined hands, and turn to face outwards and bow again.

Sekishin: Is it best that we do *Zazen* in some place that is quiet?

Gudo: Well, the quieter the better. Of course, it is not a practice only for the inside of some monastery. It is a practice for anyone and anywhere, in any circumstances, even amid the harshest noise or other conditions. However, where possible, a quite setting helps settle the mind. On a daily basis, we can do it at home, and it should be done every single day.

Sekishin: It is necessary to do it every day?

Gudo: Yes. If you do not keep at it, its goodness cannot readily manifest. Furthermore, even should a person have secluded himself or herself in some monastery for 10 or 20 days or more, practicing *Zazen* with great intensity at a *Sesshin* or the like, unless *Zazen* is continued after returning home, whatever was gained likely will be lost so very soon.

The meaning in *Zazen* is, for example, to rise in the morning and to sit before beginning one's day, finding balance in body and mind, placing the self in the same state as *Buddha* so to help spend one's entire day in that state in all one's activities. If we do not practice every day, we will keep entering and leaving, entering and leaving the state of *Buddha*, and it is possible that we will suffer psychologically even more than if we had never practiced *Zazen* at all. Thus, it is most necessary to practice *Zazen* daily as a personal life habit.

Sekishin: But it's really hard to do it every single day I think.

Gudo: Certainly, at the start, it is most difficult to get into the habit. However, to bounce back and forth between sometimes doing it and sometimes not doing it results in even more suffering. Thus, determine with all one's will to practice every day and then carry through every single day with your *Zazen*. Of course, as a beginner, things probably will not go as planned, and one will end up pausing after 3 days or so, or after 10 days or so. However, the study of Buddhism is truly a lifetime affair, and it does not matter if one falls off the horse, or off the *Zafu* cushion, so long as one gets right back on again and again, without discouragement. When it gets to the point that you are truly able to sit *Zazen* every day without resistance, you can say that you have truly entered the state of *Buddha*. When it reaches that point, by not quitting *Zazen* for one's whole life, all the problems of this life will be resolved therein. Also, when it reaches that state, should one face a day in which it is just impossible to do *Zazen*, one will feel a great sensation that something crucial is lacking from one's life, and that one almost cannot go on unless one finds a moment to do it.

Sekishin: How much time is appropriate for one sitting?

Gudo: Traditionally, the time was said to be the amount of time required for a long stick of incense to burn down, which required as much as 45 minutes. However, at the start, it is fine to begin with even 5 or 10 minutes, and to extend the time gradually as one becomes more accustomed to the practice. Because *Zazen* is a lifetime pursuit, one should just extend the time slowly, little by little.

Sekishin: And is it sufficient just to do it once per day, for example, just in the morning?

Gudo: Master Dogen wrote in his *Bendoho* that monks in a monastery should sit four times per day, in the early and late morning, in the afternoon and the evening. However, most lay people have jobs or school to attend, so I think it good to do it in the morning, as well as in the evening before bed. However, because the latter is a time when we are most tired, it may not go as well as in the morning after rising from a good sleep. Still, if one can manage to do it as the close of one's day, for even 5 or 10 minutes, it will be a good bridge into a sound sleep, and will have a huge effect to bring stability and rhythm into one's daily life.

Sekishin: I understand that *Zazen* is good before bed, but I'm just curious about the case of married individuals and sex. Would that fit in with *Zazen*?

Gudo: An interesting question! Well, I will give you a frank answer! As we discussed once before, I decided many years ago to be celibate, and I am now. However, until about 6 months before I became a priest, I continued my sexual life as a married man. I did not find a particular conflict. I recall, for example, that after love making, I might have a bit of a nice bath, followed by my *Zazen*, then off to sleep.

Sekishin: Didn't you feel some conflict in sexual passions followed by *Zazen*?

Gudo: Well, if we were to think abstractly about the matter, we might reasonably feel that there is some conflict or incongruity between the two. But, in reality, it is possible to have a time for all things, a certain time for love making, a certain time devoted to *Zazen*, and the passage of time can be something like a blade which cleanly divides the two, allowing time for all things - each in its proper time. Accordingly, an intellectual bridge can be built between these two realities, because in Buddhism we do not think by dividing this from that, lost in ideas of this and that. Rather, for lay people with home and family lives, their practice of Buddhism can encompass the total reality of the situation, and they can deal with it all in a harmonious and good manner.

ZAZEN & OUR LIVES

Just a Tiny Differance

Sekishin: In our talk a bit earlier, I heard from you that a return to our Original Self represents The Truth of Suffering level of the The Four Noble Truths, that at the level of The Truth of Accumulation there is a touching of the boundless world, and that at the stage of The Truth of Negation and Synthesis there is the idea if we do not practice it, it does not manifest. How about the fourth of The Four Noble Truths?

Gudo: We discussed on a previous day how the fourth of The Four Noble Truths, The Truth of the True Way, is centered upon *Zazen*. I believe the main issue at this stage could be phrased as the interrelationship of *Zazen* and our daily human life. Namely, when we make the practice of *Zazen* a part of our lives each morning and evening, how will that reflect itself in our daily living, and how will it become intertwined with our life?

Sekishin: Will our sitting *Zazen* have such a clearly visible effect in our day-to-day lives?

Gudo: Yes. It is so closely connected to our lives. By doing *Zazen*, the body is placed in a state of good posture and balance, and the autonomic nervous system and bodily systems are placed in balance, and thus the mind is in balance. The state of the bodymind in good balance, and of systems such as the autonomic nervous system placed in balance, is our natural and proper state. Just by our entering this state even once, such state will continue on naturally even long after we have risen from the actual sitting. Therefore, so long as that state shall continue, we shall think and feel and act in a balanced, natural and proper manner and form.

Sekishin: Can we feel the difference in ourselves between before we have begun to sit *Zazen* and after?

Gudo: You will find, gradually, great changes in your mental states and in your responses toward your life. But as a matter of fact, the natural effect of *Zazen* is that most of the key differences will *not* directly be perceived.

Sekishin: Why is that?

Gudo: For example, even should we attain a state of balance in the autonomic nervous system, it will be something outside our conscious awareness. Essentially, when we look at the autonomic nervous system as it operates internally within our bodies to regulate and control such bodily functions as heartbeat, blood circulation, digestion and such, and when we enquire as to why this system is called the *autonomic nervous system*, we find that it operates on its own, autonomously, as a system which cannot be controlled voluntarily through human will, and below the level of our usual perception. Many human systems are so. By way of example, no matter how much you might try to stop your heart just by the thought of it, it is most unlikely that you can. The same is true for your blood flow or digestive processes. You cannot do so in the same manner that you can, say, raise your arm or kick your leg merely by so willing.

The central focus of the physiological adjustments that occur through *Zazen* is in this nervous system. So, most of the changes that will have occurred within us by sitting *Zazen* will also be outside the range of our normal perception.

Sekishin: So, Roshi, are you saying these are very definite changes, but that the person doing *Zazen* may have no awareness of them?

Gudo: Yes. *Zazen* meditation has a generally good reputation for various reasons, but one cause of the fact that it is not more widely practiced among the general population is that many of the benefits are just not instant and obvious. Human beings have a foible in that, when they try something, they demand to see its effects quickly and right before their eyes. They have a tendency not to stick with something, and to quit, before the true effects manifest.

ZAZEN AT TOKEI-IN TEMPLE

Sekishin: That is for sure! Most of us try *Zazen*, and we spend much time as beginners wondering if it is having some effect or not, or about when it will have some visible effect. By the time it does, most people will have already lost patience and confidence, and shall have quit for lack of some early, instant gratification.

Gudo: The reason that I strongly recommend that *Zazen* be practiced every single day is related to that fact. In practical terms, even if someone does *Zazen*, but does it in stops and starts inconsistently, the effects may not fully manifest even after several years. On the other hand, if a person does *Zazen* daily, consistently, even if for short periods of time, within 3 months, or within 6 months, they will notice a subtle difference between the atmosphere of their life as it exists after having practiced *Zazen*, compared to the atmosphere of their life before *Zazen*. We might term this as being the difference between the World of Buddha and the World of Ordinary Men and Women. What is more, in order to notice this subtle difference, it is necessary to continue our sitting of *Zazen* every day. And, when we do come to awareness of this subtle difference, it becomes impossible for us to pause in our daily practice of *Zazen*, for it is now part of us.

Freeing Ourselves from Ideas and Conceptions

Sekishin: I understand that the benefits of daily *Zazen* might not be obvious to some, especially over the short term. But if we look at it over a longer term, it is easier to spot the effects of our practice. Isn't that right?

Gudo: That is right. As we continue over the long term, the small and subtle effects, which may not have been so immediate and obvious, will gradually build and accumulate, until it becomes absolutely clear to us that our life has changed in important ways.

Sekishin: In what ways does it change?

Gudo: First, I might say that there is a breaking away, a disengaging from ideas and conceptions. We free ourselves from the complex and entangled thinking we stir up within our heads, a maze of thought which can entrap us.

Sekishin: What do you mean by that?

Gudo: Because we can bring a balance to the autonomic nervous system and bodily systems by our sitting of morning *Zazen*, upon rising therefrom, we are able to live with composure and serenity of body, composure and serenity in mind: we can spend our day, take our breakfast, go to school, go to work, and we can engage in all activities with composure and serenity of body, composure and serenity in mind. Thereby, one effect which arises from our composure and serenity of body, our composure and serenity in mind, is a cessation of ways of thinking that pull and drag us here and there, which send the workings of our minds spinning round and round.

Sekishin: What exactly do you mean by that? What do you mean by *ways of thinking that pull and drag us here and there, sending our minds round and round*?

Gudo: When we look at our daily lives, we might say that we are made to live in a society that demands of us almost continuous thinking about all variety of matters. We find ourselves in a world in which our heads are constantly filled with thoughts, with very little opportunity to pause, very little chance to rest from all that thinking! However, such thinking can remove us and separate us from a foundation in reality, letting the mind run on and on at idle speed, in circles. The result is that much of that thinking is nothing more than a waste of time, and often it is the result that we will stumble and take many false steps in our daily lives caused thereby. Of course, the ability of the human species to think is perhaps the most important characteristic separating us from the monkeys and the other animals, and it is for this very reason that we human beings should not view lightly, should not take for granted our ability to think. However, our human ability to think can crash upon the rocks of the many weaknesses inherent in idealism, namely, that our thoughts take on a life of their own, whereby we create a fictional world, a complex and entangled world, merely by the fictions, the intricate and knotted thinking we dream up in our heads. There thus begins a state in which we are waved about, swung about by our thoughts and ideas. The harmful effects can be most grave.

171

Sekishin: And practicing *Zazen* can prevent all that from happening?

Gudo: Yes. *Zazen* has the ability … when we are just sitting without trying to think, but experience that a thought has wandered into our heads … to let us pause from that thinking, to let the thought drift from our mind. In this way, *Zazen* may be said to have the power to free us from our ideas and physical imbalances. Master Dogen stated that *Zazen* is a *dropping*, a *falling away* of body and mind. It is right to understand the falling away of body and mind as being this very freeing from ideas and physical imbalances.

Meeting Reality

Sekishin: I now understand how, as you say, *Zazen* can free us from entanglement in our own thoughts and physical imbalances, the clutter that can fill our heads and disturb the bodymind. However, I still have the impression that, when our deluded state of busy thoughts and physical imbalances vanishes, all that remains is a blank, vacant space, empty of all positive value.

Gudo: If you are asking whether our disentanglement from thoughts and conceptions is really necessary or not, well, when we look through what fills today's internet and the television, or some of the popular magazines and books in wide circulation and lining our bookshelves, all the talk in society of this and that and other nonsense, the necessity of disengaging from that tangle is something that we may feel keenly. *Zazen* is not just some passive, negative escape from our ideas and conceptions, but as the other side of the coin, has a positive, active face as well.

Sekishin: What is that positive, active face?

Gudo: That is the issue of our meeting reality head on. In leading our day-to-day lives, we often mumble platitudes about how something *is real*, or something *is truly* such and such. But these are just words expressing notions held within our heads about what is true and real. It is a world of reality as words. However, the state wherein we set ourselves down upon a sitting cushion, crossing our legs and placing our hands together in *Mudra*, making the backbone straight and upright, without an intent to think of this or to think of that … such is the state of the straight-forward, direct, and face-to-face confronting of the circumstances that encompass us and encompass all, the world which holds us and of which we are one facet, a meeting and encounter with Reality itself. It is a world that cannot be expressed by any words. It cannot be expressed in words, for it is the world supreme in size and in scope, spreading and expanding without limit, encompassing all free of limit. When we sit *Zazen*, we can meet, every single day and face-to-face, as our *True Face* that world supreme in scope, that which is all, that which takes in all without limit. Thereby, when we ask about what is reality, the answer comes not by any mere idea held in our thinking, but by direct experience with the whole body and mind, here and now, right in the very flesh.

Sekishin: What is the result?

Gudo: The result is that every single day, we are hit by the tremendous forces and power of that very world of reality which holds us, which takes us in. Our eyes are opened to the delicate subtlety, as well as the complexity, of the cause and effect relationships existing within the world of reality.

Sekishin: So, there is also some connection to things such as cause and effect?

Gudo: By our meeting and facing reality day-by-day, we find that the world of reality stands right before us, and we study all with the modesty and humbleness which human beings should possess, coming to an attitude of awe and reverence toward cause and effect.

Sekishin: What is the result of our coming to hold awe and reverence toward cause and effect?

Gudo: As our awe and reverence toward cause and effect deepens, we become ever more eager to study cause and effect. To say it in simple terms, we strive to come to a wise and proper understanding toward any matter or problem we encounter … and to say it in even simpler terms, we become most diligent students of life.

Sekishin: Is there anything else?

Gudo: Our belief in superstitions disappear, and we begin to think about things logically. For example, we often find that religious beliefs include some faith in the arising of the miraculous or in super-human powers and abilities, in souls and spirits which wander about, in worlds after death and the like. However, the philosophy of Buddhism is a stance both indifferent and unrelated to such things, and we might say that the reason Guatama Buddha appeared in this world was for the purpose of banishing all such superstitions.

Further, to the extent that persons believe in the workings of cause and effect, those persons, whether they intend to or not, will become industrious strivers in their pursuits. Those things that make us happy as human beings, and those that make us unhappy, all are dependent on our actions and conduct as human beings. When we strive industriously, we believe that there will be fruits to our striving solely by our making such effort. To the extent that a human being believes in cause and effect, we are compelled into a state of body and mind in which we must strive and make effort.

Giving Rise to an Energy for Doing

Sekishin: I pretty much understand your points about our freeing ourselves from ideas and physical imbalances, and meeting reality face-to-face. But are there any other, somewhat more practical and immediate effects from *Zazen*?

Gudo: Because the state of doing *Zazen* … or, if I may say it in other words, because the state of body and mind wherein there is balance in the autonomic nervous system and other bodily and mental systems … is a state of our acting with all we have, with all our life and energy, our sitting *Zazen* every day results in our life becoming an extremely active life. Buddhism is a philosophy very different from a life of merely sitting in some library, reading about the exploits of other people in dry books, or of merely observing from afar the doings of others as if a spectator in a theater.

Sekishin: But in this dangerous society in which we are presently living, isn't it easy for us to be hurt or exposed to risks and peril through being so active and energetic in our doings? Isn't it better just to take the tried and true, the safe road?

174

Gudo: Well, our taking our lumps and bumps is certainly a possibility. However, it is not Buddhism unless we are active in our pursuits. *Zazen* begins and ends in sitting, but that is only the beginning and *Zazen* is not about just sitting around! Accordingly, the life of the Buddhist is a life of energy and activity, although we might sometimes bump our heads.

Sekishin: Of course, we all want to avoid being hurt in life as much as possible.

Gudo: Well, avoiding a few bumps and broken bones in life in just not possible. I do not mean to say that we need love the idea of our getting hurt. What is more, from the perspective of Buddhism, it is just *impossible* that we can ever be hurt at all, even with the bumps and broken bones, for Buddhism is the Truth which encompasses and sweeps within itself all that is this world of ours, whereby when we trust in that perspective, and to the extent we settle our body and mind each day through the practice of *Zazen*, all that happens does develop, arises and falls, in accord with the order of the universe, life going as it goes. There is something which cannot be bruised or broken even as we experience life's breaks. When nothing can ever be lacking, what is there that can be harmed? Who is there to suffer harm? What to render harm? All is just the natural unfolding of events, going as it goes.

But even if we were to assume that we could, indeed, suffer some harm or injury, because the same is but an effect, a result in accordance with the order of the universe –the world just going as it needs to go – we should joyfully submit to, welcome and be accepting of it. Such submission and self-surrender will come back to us to serve as a great plus, a great strength in life.

Sekishin: But even if you say that, it really can be a terrible matter when we get badly hurt.

Gudo: Yes, I know as I have also encountered very hard times. However, human beings are strange animals, and we do not always detest all aspects of the harsh experiences we might undergo. Thus, there are people who may thrill and thrive in hard circumstances and difficult situations, who may find a meaning to their life precisely in the living of that which is not easy to live. For example, something which is sometimes talked about these days is the phenomenon of people who give up comfortable, economically prosperous lives in order to pursue some dream or calling, no matter how much they must materially sacrifice thereby. Of course, I am not referring to those people who, for example, feel they just do not conform to the job and other responsibilities they find themselves in, and thereby, for their own self-interest, blindly flee in search of a life without any constraints upon them at all. Unless they are careful, they will just keep chasing after a mirage they will never find. Sometimes, we need to realize that true freedom is not something over the distant hills, but is to be found right under our feet, here and now. However, I also cannot agree with the idea that a person simply needs to accept that society is just what it is, and its structures and restrictions are just what they are and cannot be helped, whereby we must merely dive into some dogmatic and shallow resignation to circumstances, and bury ourselves in a fraudulent life of compromise and quiet desperation.

Sekishin: And what would you recommend should be done?

Gudo: I think that every individual should prize and hold in respect the work, the tasks and like responsibilities that they now are performing. The work and tasks that you are currently engaged in are likely not something that appeared in your life merely by chance. Leading up to your currently being engaged in a certain employ, so very many cause and effect relationships, layer upon layer, one upon the other, built up and interacted to bring you there: the fact of your birth, the fact of the culture you were raised in, your family circumstances and history, your education and life experiences, and so on. Accordingly, the most Buddhist way of dealing with the job that a human being has been given, is, first, to put one's whole heart into that work, to pour all one's efforts into it. And if one were to inquire as to what direction is best for one to pour those efforts, guidance will come to you via one's daily sitting of *Zazen*. For many human beings, particularly in this competitive, capitalistic society, their work is the main place for them to vent and expend their energies, and is a great source of self-image and self-judgment too. Of course, there are many people who spend much more of their planning and energy on how they will amuse themselves after work and on the weekends, drinking and carousing and the like, much more planning and energy than they devote to their day jobs. But I do not consider that as the best way to spend these short lives we have been given, and in fact, it strikes me as a great waste of our time. We must remember that our lives are just these very

176

circumstances we face before us. Thus, sometimes we may elect to stick to our duties and obligations as the best course, while at other times we may choose to make a change and to leave our duties and obligations behind as the best course. Yet, in either staying or leaving, there is truly no place we go. All is ever what we face before us, all is ever just this very place where we stand in life.

TOKEI-IN TEMPLE, SHIZUOKA, JAPAN

Home Leaving, Home Staying

Sekishin: So, Roshi, the subject of our careers and working life just came up. Do you think that it is therefore possible for someone to continue their work and career, while simultaneously leading a life in Buddhism?

Gudo: Absolutely. Yes! People who have jobs out in the general society can pursue *Zazen* hand-in-hand therewith. And, it is exactly in such a situation that the true meaning and value of *Zazen* manifests.

177

Sekishin: However, if I recall correctly, Master Dogen emphasized in the *Shobogenzo* that it is necessary for the seeker to leave home so to attain Truth.

Gudo: Of course, when persons are seeking to engage in intensive Buddhist training, especially training to become a Zen priest, it is possible that those people instead will become attached to family and home, and need to avoid becoming overly caught up and dragged around by the demands of the world, demands which could interfere with the necessary focus on one's training. Accordingly, Buddhist training can appear to have a cold and heartless aspect to it, asking one to cut ties to home and family and such. However, we must keep in mind that this real world in which we are living can sometimes be a tough, cold and heartless place, and to study the realities of that world, it perhaps may be necessary to also adopt and hold fast to an unemotional, seemingly cold stance toward the world sometimes, at least from certain perspectives, and for certain periods in training

Sekishin: Is that the perspective behind the idea that Buddhist priests should be home leavers, should leave home for purposes of Buddhist training?

Gudo: Yes. If circumstances permit, it is traditionally thought best that the trainee leave home. However, from another perspective, this leaving home can be viewed as but another form of selecting and dedicating oneself to a career. So, it may not be the best path for everyone, or in all cases. Furthermore, if everyone in society were simultaneously to decide to pack it all in to become celibate monks in monasteries, well, our society would collapse very fast! Thereby, I find it perfectly natural that there should be some people who, as a part of their Buddhist training, continue to engage in their ordinary careers and lives. All can be an element of training. I believe that some Buddhist priests should live alone in hermits caves or huts in isolated and distant mountains, that other Buddhist priests should devote themselves full time to life in a monastery or in a temple, but that many other Buddhist priests should live out in the world, knowing the world and the nature of life with family and in general society. All such Buddhists can have something of great value to teach, can find their own unique ways to practice and express their Buddhism, can offer their own important perspectives on Buddhism.

Sekishin: But I would think that such practitioners who live out in the world, with all its great demands … I would think such people are losing whatever chance they might have had to attain *Satori*.

Gudo: Ah! Finally, this topic of *Satori* has risen its head! I think you really want to ask what *Satori* means, what is this attainment of *Satori*, this *Enlightenment* that gets shouted about. I sometimes joke that Guatama Buddha used to employ wondrous sounding phrases such as *Satori* and the like simply in order to make his teachings a bit more interesting sounding! (*chuckling*) And when people use the term to mean falling for a time into some strange or abnormal mental state, like something that might be caused by sleep deprivation or a denial of proper nutrition or drugs or hypnosis, which is often the case in monastery life, by the way, well, that is a type of farce as well. There is nothing that causes a greater misunderstanding about Buddhism, nothing that causes a greater misunderstanding about *Zazen*.

Sekishin: Are you saying that there is no such thing as *Satori*?

ZENDO OF THE TOKEI-IN

Gudo: If you understand some points about *Satori* that often have been misinterpreted by some, you will find that such experiences can manifest in life hundreds, thousands, any number of times in our lives. In Buddhism, the meaning of *Satori* is nothing more, nothing less than the state of the body, the state of the mind in *Wisdom* when we are doing *Zazen*. Accordingly, anybody, any person, just by the fact that they are sitting *Zazen*, can immediately and directly enter and attain the state of *Satori*. This is why Master Dogen stated, "*[A] beginner's pursuit of the truth is just the whole body of the original state of experience.*" A person who is sitting *Zazen*, no matter who that person is, should think of himself or herself as already thus attained of the state of Buddha.

ZENDO OF THE TOKEI-IN

180

Sekishin: So, if we sit *Zazen* in the morning, we … any such person … can think of himself or herself as being in the state of Buddha all day long? It is both when we are sitting and when we get up from sitting?

Gudo: In principle, it is fine to think in that way. Even an instant of *Zazen* is Buddha realized, a fact which is so even as we rise from sitting and get on with all the rest of life. But, even so, we must not neglect sitting. Thus, as not too big an interval exists in our practice, I recommend that it is best to practice *Zazen* every day, in both the morning and at night.

Sekishin: Do I understand correctly that, just by the fact that a person can sit *Zazen* every day, in the morning and at night, *Satori* has already been attained thereby?

Gudo: Yes, when one correctly understands that it is so, it becomes so. By the sitting of *Zazen*, in the morning and in the evening, the state of Buddha continues throughout the day and in every instant. And by doing it every day, the state of Buddha continues all one's lifetime. To the extent that *Zazen* is faithfully engaged in every day without fail, then it shall have become impossible to depart from the state of being Buddha even should one try to do so. In fact, we are always in the state of Buddha, but this daily practice of *Zazen* helps us realize and manifest what was so all along yet hidden to our eyes, as bodymind attains the balance and *Wisdom* of Buddha.

Sekishin: Can we thus say that the target of our Buddhist practice becomes to continue the sitting of *Zazen*, both in the morning and in the night, every single day without ceasing?

Gudo: Yes. And to manifest this in all one's life too. If one reaches the point of being able to sit *Zazen* every day, at the start of the day and at the end, then we can say that our training in Buddhist practice has been fully accomplished and made complete. One can then bring this into all life. Whether a home leaver or a home stayer, it is all the same. By simply having acquired that ability, there is not one thing missing, not one more goal to aim toward, nothing more to attain. If the practice of *Zazen*, morning and night, is continued for a lifetime, one will end one's life, one will die as, oneself, the Buddha.

181

Questions of Life and Death

Sekishin: The subject of death has come up. Roshi, may I ask your opinion on life after death? Do you believe in some form of life after death?

Gudo: Well, what do you mean by life after death?

Sekishin: Well, what is typical in most religions is to say, for example, that after the death of our earthly body, the soul or spirit goes on living, to be reborn in some other world or form.

Gudo: If that is what is meant, then I must say, no, I do not believe in such things.

Sekishin: Why is that?

Gudo: My reasoning stems from one basic principle of Buddhist philosophy, namely, the *Oneness of Body and Mind*, the *Oneness of Mind and Phenomena*. Accordingly, in Buddhism, it is not proper to think that the physical body and the mind can be divided into two, that the spirit and physical phenomena are two separate things. Therefore, our psychological and mental functioning is directly intertwined with all our bodily functions: blood circulation, the diffusion of oxygen via the lungs, the activity of the brain cells, etc. Thus, from the standpoint of Buddhist philosophy, it is just not permitted for us to believe that, at the stage at which blood flow, respiration, the activity of the brain cells and the like shall all have ceased, somehow our mental existence continues on.

Sekishin: However, it is the common belief that Buddhism recognizes some existence after death, perhaps some form of rebirth, and that is why Buddhist priests are so often engaged in performing funeral services, memorial services for the dead, and the like.

Gudo: It is true that most people picture Buddhism as containing doctrines of reincarnation or rebirth or some other life after death. But, these ideas stem from

182

teachings of Brahmanism, which existed in ancient India long before the time of the advent of Buddhism, teachings which were mixed into Buddhism in the process of Buddhist beliefs developing in India and being transplanted and propagated from India to other regions and cultures of the world. In fact, beliefs in some life after death as asserted in Brahmanistic teachings did not occupy a central place in early Buddhism as much as people sometimes assume. In reality, we who are living cannot know for sure whether there is or is not some ongoing life after death. There may be such things, or there may not. Thus, we had best focus on this very life we do have, here and now, just living fully the life before us. If we focus on being a true human being in this very life we are living, what may or may not come after will take care of itself.

ZENDO OF THE TOKEI-IN

Sekishin: But all people fear death, which is why many will most likely be shocked when they hear that there may be nothing after death.

Gudo: Yes. That is true. However, to invent some world after this life just to placate people's fears is a great wrong, I believe, committed by those who assert its existence.

Sekishin: To deny the existence of life after death … Is that not to fall into a way of thinking which Guatama Buddha indicated as incorrect, namely, that there are no *Karmic* relationships, no relationships of cause and effect in this world?

Gudo: To deny the existence of life after death is *not* the same thing as denying the existence of cause and effect. In fact, precisely because we should strongly believe in the existence of cause and effect, we thus cannot seek for some way of thinking in which the spirit pops out of the physical body at death, and comes to live in some other world or state.

Sekishin: So how should we deal with our fears about death?

Gudo: With regard to that subject, Master Dogen provided us a clear solution in the *Shobogenzo* by quoting the words of the Chinese teacher, Master Yuanwu Keqin (Master Engo Kokugon in Japanese).

Sekishin: What was that clear solution?

Gudo: What Master Kokugon said was, *"Life is the manifestation of all functions, Death is the manifestation of all functions."* The meaning is that, when we are living, there is just life and nothing else. We should live with all our heart and being, we should live as if our very life depended on it! And when we die, there is just death and nothing else. We should just die with all our heart and being, dying right to the very death!

Sekishin: That is a pretty harsh sounding idea, and a very intense teaching!

Gudo: However, life can be rather harsh. The real world is often most intense! Because our lives can be harsh and intense, it does not help anyone merely to teach them that

184

they should always relax and simply take life easy. Sometimes, life must be lived actively, with strength and firm resolve, for the circumstances might demand nothing less!

Sekishin: However, in the end, life is just an ephemeral thing, fleeting and ultimately coming all to naught. Is that the point?

Gudo: No, that is *not* the case! First, it only comes to naught when we try to live by, always, always, taking it easy in the world, for such a world does not really exist. Further, an awareness that we cannot have expectations of some life after death should lead us to realize that we must really live to the fullest in this life that we have, here and now. This very moment by moment, here and now, that has been granted to us who are alive, packs all the meaning of all eternity in each instant. Open your eyes, and find that life continues on and on in each blade of grass, bird and fish and child's breath and, as Master Dogen heard, in tiles and pebbles, mountains and waters too. How then can it be fleeting and ephemeral? Asking ourselves in each and every moment how we should live in that moment, this is the one and only source for bestowing meaning in our lives.

X. ENDINGS

JUST WHAT GOOD IS BUDDHISM, REALLY?

Sekishin: In our talks, Roshi, I heard from you so many novel perspectives regarding points of Buddhist philosophy, points that I would not even have thought to consider before our discussions. Some of your ideas really hit me straight away, and I was persuaded right off by your comments. On some other points, however, well, I must admit that I still find some things a bit harder to swallow, and I know that I need to make further study of those to truly understand.

One issue that still remains for me, Roshi, and that I feel very keenly, is the doubt I hold about just what good all these ideas of Buddhist philosophy actually are, just what role they serve in this present age and society. Just what good is Buddhism, really?

Of course, these are religious issues, so maybe I should not ask about purpose, or think from such a utilitarian standpoint. But, after all, when we just look at these things, I don't believe that we can help but to ask these questions of utility and purpose from time to time, to ask just what good it all serves. So, I would like you to say something about the meaning and true significance of Buddhism in this modern world.

Gudo: Well, just as you say, because Buddhism is a form of religion, perhaps we shouldn't look at these questions for their utilitarian value alone. On the other hand, Buddhism does serve a clear purpose: we study Buddhism because we see it as a unique statement of Truth in the world, a valid explanation of the way the world is. We also come to it because we see that it may have some relationship to bringing about human well-being in life. On a practical level, let us suppose that Buddhism were not helpful in contributing to well-being in our lives, in leading human beings to a good

187

path for the leading of their lives. Would we not then be left to wonder just how true and useful it might actually be after all? So, I would like to focus on this issue for a moment: the question of what Buddhism contributes to our lives as individuals ...

The Individual & Buddhism

Sekishin: What meaning does Buddhism offer to the individual person?

Gudo: I have heard you say many times that our modern society has become more and more controlling and restraining of individual freedom in life, that the degree of control and restraint is becoming ever greater and more oppressive, while our ability to find our own meaning and path in life is becoming narrower and narrower in turn. Is that what you believe?

ZEN FOR A MODERN WORLD

Sekishin: Yes. And I don't just come to that conclusion on a theoretical level, for our busy work lives and the other societal demands upon us are taking ever greater and greater amounts of our time, energy and devotion. We are slaves to the system. I feel this very strongly.

Gudo: Modern society, and the demands of the modern economy, make it hard to deny what you are saying. So many people are being forced to become slaves to the jobs and other demands that society is placing upon them. It is a worldwide trend in capitalist countries, I believe.

Sekishin: And because we don't want to be labeled as rebels and trouble makers, or to bear the hardships of being outsiders in society, ending up on the unemployment line, for example, so many of us just bite our tongues and go along with the system, sacrificing our own will and desires, never spreading our own wings. We compromise, and compromise again in quiet desperation, but always wondering if our current road is really the path we should have followed.

Gudo: Yes. If there is a necessity for religion, it is right there. Right at the start of our talks, I mentioned that religion is actually but a question for each of us regarding what personal outlook, just what way of thinking, we will select in viewing life and the world. It is a selection which none of us can avoid because we all have to choose some worldview, the manner in which we will think about life and our place in it. So, we all must choose a religion of some kind, even if that religion is, we think, the belief that we are not religious. The particular religion we each choose is related to the issue you bring up: the modern society in which we are living is a place of some instability and unease for the individual, who can often feel oppressed by its demands. One reason is that the respective individuals who constitute society may not possess, for themselves, clear standards regarding how the individual should govern and discipline his or her own life. In other words, they have not fully developed for themselves some fundamental philosophy and touchstone way of thinking, some clear religious view. The void left by their failure to have a fundamental and solid philosophy is one cause of the problem, one cause of their feeling adrift and lost at sea, battered by the winds and tides which life throws at them.

When the individual does not have a clear religious view, a clear philosophy on life and the world, then there come to the fore overriding concerns about the individual's own status and power, economic standing and other measures of how one ranks up compared to one's fellow human beings. When we have no confidence within ourselves about just who we are, no clear philosophy which allows us to know for sure our own value, we tend to feel insecure, and to try to value ourselves by how we compare to others, such as by how much money we have in the bank. People end up being all caught up and dragged about by such petty concerns and comparisons. Most people do not possess the strength truly to resist and be critical of such a state of affairs. They merely go along with the herd mentality, following blindly in the same direction as everyone else, each one thinking for their own self-interest, scrambling and competing with all the others to be on top. The result is that societal disorder and confusion spread widely; human uncertainty and anxiety are on the rise.

Sekishin: So, are you saying that part of the solution for this situation is for each of the individuals who make up society to possess a clear personal philosophy, a clear religion?

MASTER NISHIJIMA's 4 VOLUME ENGLISH TRANSLATION
(with Chodo Cross) OF THE *SHOBOGENZO*

Gudo: Yes. So long as the individual men and women who constitute society do not have a clear idea of by what standards they should best live their lives, and so long as they just go around and around, right and left, keeping an eye cast sideways on what everybody else is doing, well, so long as that is so, there is no expectation for resolving so many of the problems that are caused in society precisely by that state of affairs.

Sekishin: In recent decades, many young people from America, Europe and other westernized countries have taken up an interest in Buddhism, *Zazen* and such. Is this phenomenon related to the human insecurities you have just expressed?

Gudo: Over the years, I have met so many young westerners, not to mention young Japanese, who have come to me with an interest in Buddhism and *Zazen*, and I believe that the root issue with most of them is just what I described. In the case of the westerners, so many of them come to Japan thinking that they will find in Japanese or Asian culture something that will serve to help resolve their internal discord and discomfort. I tell them that the indispensable method for them to follow in seeking resolution is simply to pursue their study of Buddhism … to sit *Zazen*.

Society & Buddhism

Sekishin: I pretty much understand the importance of religion, including Buddhism, to the individual, but could you speak a bit more about the relationship of Buddhism to larger social problems?

Gudo: Yes. The society in which we are now living is a capitalistic system, wherein there co-exists the constant need for us to sell our labor on a daily basis, in combination with our desire to take the fruits and wages therefrom in order to live some life of gorgeous consumerism and consumption which, society tell us, is the so-called good life. This cycle of our work to raise funds, followed by our using those funds to buy things, certainly has given rise to various material advantages in our lives and in society, all the comforts of the modern economy and its wealth. But it can also lead to certain spiritual disadvantages. We can be torn by divergent ways of thinking, ways of

191

feeling and calls to action within ourselves, as the need for material gain leads us one way, although our heart might best lead us another. Now, this is not just a problem for the individual, but for society as a whole.

Because we do not know any other way of life, because we are addicted to consumerism, we have all bought into this system of buying: we strive and strive to purchase, not only things we truly need, but so much that is truly wasteful, things we do not need at all. The result is damage, not only to our environmental resources, but to ourselves as well when our happiness comes to hang upon the latest trinket we have bought. We do not know when we already have enough, for society feeds us the message that we must keep buying, working, consuming and buying more, without end. Further, we are divided into those who have too much, and those who do not have even the basics necessities of life. I do not think that this organization for our society is the best way to go about things.

SPEAKING TO YOUNG PEOPLE AROUND THE WORLD

The system is supported because of the self-centered thinking and self-interested pursuits of the people who constitute the society. Still, many people know on some level that something is wrong with this state of affairs. Most people, even while

192

constantly thinking about maintaining and protecting their own economic profit and their own societal advantages, and even while believing that the current system which they have a stake in deserves their respect and allegiance, most such people also, on some level, instinctually have belief in the need for a less materialistic value system and point of view. Accordingly, they also recognize that something in the system needs fixing and that many of the criticisms leveled against the system as it presently exists are not wrong. That does not mean, of course, that blind criticism of the system, or the desire to tear it all down and start again, is right either. Perhaps what is required is a viewpoint somewhere in between, a *Middle Way* of thinking about the content and functioning of capitalist society.

Sekishin: And, Roshi, you believe that such a viewpoint, such a middle stance, is provided by Buddhism?

Gudo: Yes. I hope you have understood from our talks so far that I see the philosophy of Buddhism as a return to our most fundamental nature, a return causing us to reexamine and reappraise the world, this reality which holds us and from which we are never apart. In this same way, I hope that the philosophy of Buddhism will allow us to reexamine and reappraise the opposing viewpoints concerning our modern society I mentioned, to find a middle ground between viewpoints which fully support the system and viewpoints fully critical of it.

Sekishin: Specifically, how?

Gudo: Well, specifically, let's take those people who unqualifiedly support our present society and economic system, who think primarily about their personal advantages and disadvantages, profits and demerits. It helps such persons to see that support for the current system, from a spiritual perspective, also has many disadvantages and demerits. It helps those persons to see the weakness and fragility of the foundation upholding their support. No less, it helps those people who unqualifiedly criticize our present society and economic system to see that they need to be careful about dreams of some utopia, or ideas of some revolution or other radical or extremist change to the world.

Sekishin: So, people at both extremes need to coolly reappraise their views on reality.

Gudo: Exactly right. If both sides do not cool down, and if each side just continues to fight all out to impose its political views on society, it all will come to nothing and be a great waste of effort and energy. No real fruit will come of it.

Sekishin: You can say much the same thing about our political parties and most politicians.

Gudo: That is right. These days, the parties on the left and the parties on the right in Western countries seem to have drawn near in their positions, and sometimes, to have switched places. Unfortunately, the reason is not out of some spirit of compromise and working together. It is more a matter of politicians without real conviction, mostly concerned with their own reelection and backers, who take the safe road that pleases the greatest number of constituent voters. People seem generally disillusioned with the political system, which appears to have value only in how it can be used to provide various vested societal interests with economic advantages or disadvantages.

Sekishin: Both the extreme right and the extreme left seem to be fading, and political power has become clustered in the middle. Is this related to what you mean?

Gudo: The fact that the extreme right and the extreme left seem to be fading, and political power is now clustered in the middle in economically developed countries is a desirable thing from some points of view, when it entails compromise and a common vision for society. But to the extent that there is lacking a definite ideological system behind this merging in the center, it is still just a matter of politics being used, not for compromise, but to fight over how the pie is divided up among the various economic and political special interest groups in the society. If that is the case, the end result could even be an ultimate revival of extremism in the future.

Sekishin: I think you have in mind something like what happened in Germany after World War I where, when the political parties and political system failed to properly function at a time of social crisis, it paved the way for the rise of extremists such as the Nazis.

Gudo: Unfortunately, yes. The same phenomenon happened in Japan during that period. Both political stability and social stability are grounded in ideological stability, and the possession of healthy religious, balanced philosophical views in that society. That is extremely important.

International Society & Buddhism

Sekishin: Besides questions of domestic politics, how do you see these issues from an international point of view?

Gudo: When I think of these things from an international perspective, the major problem facing the world today is the conflict between Western societies and religious extremism of all kinds, including, but not limited to by any means, Islamic extremism. Both sides believe that their particular views are proper, and both sides seek to make their values the dominant value system by destroying the other. However, I cannot but criticize any form of extremism that seeks to take away the liberty that does exist, however imperfectly, in Western society. The points of view of the religious extremists do not appear to allow much room for compromise with the rest of the world that does not share their creed. It is unlikely that both groups can live together in peace, and violence will keep occurring. We also face the presence of terrible weapons of mass destruction spread around the world. That threat hangs over us night and day.

One very small thing that can be done from the perspective of Buddhism is to criticize any ideology of extremism, be it extreme idealism or extreme materialism, and to develop, from a higher vantage point, a world view based on a Middle Way. We can try to persuade one person at a time of the value in doing so. In order for the human race to survive in this 21st Century, all people need to learn to speak to each other from such a position of openness and tolerance in resolving the issues between them.

DHARMA TRANSMISSION
TO FURTHER GENERATIONS OF ZEN TEACHERS

Sekishin: And you think that religious beliefs such as those of Buddhism offer such a middle position, such a middle world view, based on openness and tolerance?

Gudo: It may just be my own perspective, but when I look at the course of world history, and at the present state of the world, and when I think from the logic and higher perspective of Buddhism, I cannot doubt that such a viewpoint will become a centerpiece of discussion as the 21st Century progresses, if we are to survive as a world.

196

A FINAL CUP OF TEA ...

Sekishin: Roshi, nothing in this world is permanent, and thus these talks of ours must draw to an end for now. I have so enjoyed our many days together, and I hope that there are many more in the future as well. May I ask you if there is anything that you might add in conclusion to all we have covered?

Gudo: If I were to say one last thing, it is that I believe that we are standing right in the middle of a world that desperately needs the perspectives of Buddhism.

Sekishin: Do you think that is happening, that the world is slowing coming around to the perspectives of Buddhism?

Gudo: It is a very quiet process, not too visible to the eye, but I think that the influence of Buddhism is gradually spreading throughout many quarters of society, and is having many good effects.

Sekishin: But isn't it necessary for Buddhism to be rediscovered in the right way, and to spread through society in a proper form?

Gudo: Certainly. That is right. However, if we look at the forms of Buddhism which are spreading widely, we see that there are a great variety of forms which have not yet become unified into an ideological whole, and that over the long history of Buddhism, there have been fostered within Buddhism more than a few harmful aspects and tendencies. In fact, there has only been some very little progress toward a true reconstruction and reform within Buddhism.

Sekishin: And what would be the most important factor for that reconstruction and reform to finally happen within Buddhism?

Gudo: The factor more important than any other is for as many people as possible to begin to engage in *Zazen.* That is the most important thing. In that way, Buddhism will not be a matter of mere words and theory, or superstitious beliefs, but will be tasted and experienced right in the flesh, right through our own bodies and minds.

Sekishin: But, that is a very difficult undertaking to bring to fruition.

Gudo: It certainly is. However, unless simple and modest efforts are made in that direction, and unless Buddhism in its true meaning is revived through means of its actual practice, then no revival of Buddhism in its true meaning will be possible at all.

Sekishin: It sounds as if we who engage in *Zazen* bear a great mission!

Gudo: Well, yes, I would say that. We are up against a most difficult task. But it has to be done, and if it is not done by us, then who will do so? It may be our responsibility w that we bear to the future of Buddhism. Our efforts may be small, but still, we are making the efforts that we make. So, I would like to end this talk with the simple wish that as many people as possible, people with heart, will come to join us in this effort, will come to sit *Zazen*.

Sekishin: Thank you, Roshi, for all your wise words. May we end our discussions by sitting *Zazen* together.

Gudo: Yes. Let us now sit.

Gudo Wafu Nishijima Roshi

APPENDIX I

PROFILE & TALK by REMPO NIWA ZENJI

Zuigaku Rempo Niwa Zenji
瑞岳丹羽廉芳禅師

By all accounts, Nishijima Roshi's Teacher, Zuigaku Rempo Niwa Zenji, was a sweet, tender and caring man. Niwa Zenji was the Seventy-Seventh Abbot of Eiheiji Monastery, the temple of Dogen Zenji. (In fact, the honorific "Zenji" is granted in the Soto School to those few who have been the Abbots of Eiheiji or Sojiji, the two senior monasteries of Soto Zen in Japan). Niwa Zenji subsequently served as the Chief Abbot of the Soto School (Kancho), the official head of the sect, and was granted by the Japanese Emperor the honorific title "Jikô Enkai Zenji" ("Great Zen Master of Compassionate Light, Ocean of Plenitude"; 慈光圓海禅師). A Grand Master of "Baika" Buddhist hymn singing and a recognized master of calligraphy, many of his brushed works appear under pen names such as "Old Plum" (老梅), "Snow Plum" (雪梅) and others.

205

Calligraphy by Rempo Niwa Zenji
Great Way Gateless (大道無門)

Niwa Zenji was born on February 23rd, 1905, the sixth of ten children of Kataro (father) and Mura (mother) Shionoya in Uryuno Village, Kimizawa County, Shizuoka Prefecture, Japan. In 1916, by his own request at only the tender age of 12, a "Homeleaving" Priest Ordination was performed by his uncle, Niwa Butsuan Roshi (丹羽佛庵老師) of the Tokei-in Temple (洞慶院) in Shizuoka. Niwa Zenji would remain a priest for the next 77 years, until his death. He recounted the story in his memoirs:

At the age of twelve, my grandfather's 7th Annual Memorial Service was conducted by Rev. Kagashima Sojun of the Jotokuin and the priest who would eventually become my master, Rev. Niwa Butsuan. My Master, Butsuan, was the second son of my grandfather Kishiro, and so my father Kataro's first younger brother. Butsuan had received Homeleaving Ordination under Rev. Niwa Bukkan of the Ryuunin, the Dragon Cloud Temple, in what is now Shimizu City in Shizuoka, and Butsuan was then the Head Priest of the Tokei-in Temple in Shizuoka.

I recall that the purple color of the Kesa robe my Master wore at the Memorial Service was wonderful, and enchanted me and made me truly want to wear such a Kesa. I thought, "I want to become a Buddhist Priest too!" That evening, when all my relatives were gathered around the cooking hearth, I came right out and said so. My father agreed, saying, "I see. Because there are so many children, Ren, shall we ask Uncle's temple to do this for us?" But my mother, Mura, spoke against it, pleading, "Even before this boy had entered primary school, he already was helping me in gathering mulberries for the silkworms, making Udon noodles, carrying rice to the miller. We have ten children, but I just can't be apart from this one."

But in the end, after being persuaded by my relatives, my mother reluctantly agreed.

My Master, Butsuan, welcomed it and declared, "This is to be celebrated, even our Founder Dogen Zenji was only 14 years old when he was Ordained!" In my childish heart, I thought, "Wow, I am going to become a monk at about the same age as Dogen!", and I still remember how excited I was as if it were just yesterday.

Following that day, I got my wicker bags together, and I set out the next afternoon for Shizuoka. It was 1916, April 8th, and I was in the 6th grade of elementary school.

～ From Niwa Rempo's Book, 「The Plum Flower Opens – My Life Until Now 梅華開－わが半生」～

Niwa Butsuan Roshi
丹羽仏庵老師

    Upon Ordination, he received the monk's name Zuigaku Rempô, meaning "Auspicious Mountain-Peak, Pure Fragrance" and in 1926, at age 22, received Dharma Transmission from Niwa Butsuan Roshi. Soon after, he began study at Tokyo Imperial University (now The University of Tokyo) majoring in Indian Philosophy, and following graduation, returned to Toukei-in Temple to serve as the Kansu (監寺) temple supervisor. In October 1933, at age 29, he completed his time in the Monk's Hall at Eiheiji, and returned to the Tokei-in.

The Tôkei-in is considered the root temple of our Lineage through Niwa Zenji, Butsuan Roshi and earlier Ancestors. It has been a Zen temple of the Soto school since the 15th Century, and is located in the beautiful green hills near to the town of Shizuoka (180 km to the west of Tokyo) on Mt. Kuzumi. In fact, Niwa Zenji's connection to Tokei-in continued throughout his life, right until his eventual death in one of its pavillions. In April 1936, at age 32, Niwa Zenji was officially appointed as Lecturing Instructor for Soto Zen Doctrine (宗乗担当講師) accompanying the opening of the Monk's Training Hall at Tokei-in. The opening of the Training Hall was an important event for the temple. Although officially ranked as a "Daijuu Zenrin," one of the "ten great monasteries" of Soto Zen in Japan, and a "Senmon Sodo," a temple specifically designated for the training of novice priests, the number of Priests in residence has never been great and the size of the temple always modest. Its fortunes have waxed and waned through history as well, and Niwa Zenji worked very hard during his life for its revival and present health. The opening of the Monk's Training Hall was an important step in that revival.

Spring at Tokei-in

Niwa Zenji's name only became "Niwa" some years after he first became a priest. In December 1939, at age 35, Zenji was registered in his uncle and Master's Niwa family registry, as an adopted child, changing his family surname from "Shionoya" to "Niwa." He explained:

Following in the footsteps of my Master, my surname was changed from Shionoyo to Niwa in December, 1939. Eshu (慧宗), my younger brother apprentice, left for the war, saying "If I die in the war, I would like to come home bearing the Niwa name". Our Master said, "Since you [Eshu] are my latest apprentice, it does not make sense for me to include you alone as a Niwa. First, I will register Ren, and then include Eshu under Ren's registry". In this way, the Master registered us. Eshu was made the grandson.

Looking at it from the standpoint of our Master, he was getting on in years, and even if Eshu returned from the war unhurt, the Master thought that he himself might already no longer be living. So, I think at that time he felt grandmotherly concern that I be there in the future to look after things.

However, Eshu did not return alive.

He ended up being sacrificed in a meaningless war.

In his memoirs, Niwa Zenji recounts other hardships encountered during the war, including Tokei-in's housing great numbers of school children as refugees during the worst days of the American bombing.

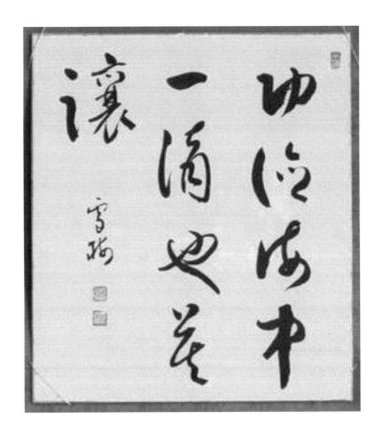

Signed as Setsubai, 雪梅, Snow Plum

Do not miss even one drop in the ocean of merit (a quote from Eihei Shingi)

210

In 1960, at age 56, Niwa Zenji was appointed the Director (Kan-In) of the Eiheiji Betsuin Training Temple, Eiheiji Monastery's branch in Tokyo, where he would remain for many years. It was there that he would eventually Ordain Gudo Nishijima. Nishijima Roshi, who was a family and working man, recalled how Niwa Zenji was willing to encourage and nurture Soto Zen Priests who would combine priesthood with lives primarily out in the world.

By the time I was 16 years old, I had already begun to have much interest in Master Dogen's Buddhist thought, especially in Shobogenzo, which I would then go on to study for many decades. Eventually, I began to translate Master Dogen's Shobogenzo from the old Japanese language into modern Japanese. This was finally published as "Gendaigoyaku Shobogenzo" or "Shobogenzo in Modern Japanese," and at that same time, I began a series of lectures on Shobogenzo at several places including the Young Men's Buddhist Association of Tokyo Imperial University [now Tokyo University] and elsewhere.

At that time I made up my mind to become a Buddhist monk in the Soto Sect but, unfortunately, as a working man supporting a wife and child, I did not feel I could abandon them to undertake monk's training for long years. I hoped to find a way to combine priesthood with my other responsibilities. Furthermore, I felt very keenly that Master Dogen's Teaching should be available to people out in the world, and not only to those leading a monastic life. Therefore, it was necessary for me to find a Buddhist Master who would permit me to become a Buddhist monk under such circumstances. Fortunately, I recalled the name of Abbot Rempo Niwa, who happened to have graduated years earlier from the same school as me, the Shizuoka Governmental High School, and I asked to visit.

I visited the Master at the Tokyo Branch of Eiheiji, and I asked to become a Buddhist monk by him. I explained my situation and my hope to unify priesthood with family, work and a beneficial life in the world. Upon hearing my story, I was joyously permitted to become a monk by him. When he listened to my proposal and wish for becoming a Buddhist monk, I noticed that he shed a little bit of tears in his eyes, and he had to wipe them. So I felt that it might also be a joyful fact for him to have me as his monk, and that he understood very well. I received Shukke Tokudo Ordination in December, 1973, next Hossen Shiki and then Dharma Transmission in 1977. From that time, Master Niwa was very kind and always careful for me not to meet any kind of difficulty in my secular job and responsibilities while continuing my Buddhist activities.

After having the ceremony to become a Buddhist monk formally, I began to teach people Zazen and Shobogenzo, even in the Tokyo Eiheiji Branch too. And because it was held every Thursday afternoon, I finished my job a little earlier than usual, and went to the temple wearing a common business suit as an ordinary salaried man. Therefore, taking off my coat, and wearing the Kashaya [Buddhist Kesa robe] over a white dress shirt, I gave my Buddhist lecture in the temple. However, some Buddhist monks in the temple thought that it was very inadequate for a Buddhist monk to hold a Buddhist lecture wearing a Kashaya over a western white dress shirt, and so they asked Master Niwa to stop such an informal style in the temple. To this Master Rempo Niwa said, "It is not so bad, because he seems to be like an Indian monk," and so I could continue my Buddhist lecture in the temple without changing my style.

Eventually I began to lead Sesshin in the temple at the end of Summer, and at that time, of course, I wore the formal black clothes of the Buddhist monk. Also, at The Buddhist Association of Tokyo University, and so forth, I used the formal Buddhist clothes as a monk without fail. Then I began to lead Sesshin in Master Rempo Niwa's temple called Tokei-in. I led Sesshin at Tokei-in six times a year, for Japanese participants sometimes and for foreign participants in English sometimes. Our relationship continued even after Master Niwa became the 77th Abbot of Eihei-ji from April 1985 to September 1993, right until his death.

I was taught so much by the Abbot Rempo Niwa about how I shall live as a human being. The Abbot Rempo Niwa was a very sensitive and generous person. … When I visited him in his private room, he sometimes served me a cup of green tea that he himself prepared. At that time, even when he did not teach me especially with words, I was able to gain so much knowledge simply by watching his behavior. He showed me at that time so many teachings.

On June 25, 1976, at age 72, Niwa Zenji was elected Assistant Abbot of Eiheiji Head Monastery, and in January 1985, at the age of 81, he became the 77th Abbot of Eiheiji. In that role, and concerned for the internationalization of Soto Zen abroad, Niwa Zenji made overseas trips to China, Europe, America and elsewhere, and oversaw the founding of an International Division at Eiheiji. Niwa Zenji gave Dharma Transmission to Master Nishijima with knowledge and encouragement of his work in Japan with both Japanese and foreigners and, among his other Dharma Heirs, bestowed Dharma Transmission on students of Taizen Deshimaru, the Teacher so influential in the propagation of Soto Teachings in Europe. On February 22, 1992, Niwa Zenji was elected the Chief Abbot of the Soto Sect, and thus formal head of the Sect.

212

Signed as Robai, 老梅, Old Plum

Snowy night in the deep mountains in my grass hut (**From a poem by Master Dogen**)

213

Calligraphy by Rempo Niwa Zenji
No Obstacles

On September 7, 1993, Niwa Zenji passed away in the Abbot's Residence known as the Plum Viewing Pavillion at the Tokei-in Temple in Shizuoka. He was 89 years old.

NIWA ZENJI ON ZEN PRACTICE

(Adapted from a 1977 interview on the NHK TV series "The Religion Hour")

The Buddha Way is to probe and see through this self, and the basis for doing so is to Practice through this human body which our self possesses. Thus, it is most vital to make effort oneself in the manner of Shakyamuni Buddha. ... In the Genjo Koan, Master Dogen speaks of "*To learn the self*":

To learn Buddhism is to learn ourself. To learn ourself is to forget ourself. To forget ourself is to be experienced by millions of things and phenomena. To be experienced by millions of things and phenomena is to let our own body and mind, and the body and mind of the external world, fall away. Then we can forget the mental trace of realization, and show the real signs of forgotten realization continually, moment by moment.

What is this word "self" of that phrase "*to learn Buddhism is to learn ourself?*" This "self" means our ordinary way of seeing things, our small self in our usual thinking. However, if we probe a little deeper beyond the "self" of our ordinary thinking, there is to be found a higher degree of self that presents a limitless interpenetration of wisdom and benevolence. If we are speaking of the ordinary self, we may come to think of just our small, deluded self as our self. But in reality, the self is noble, and if we polish it, limitless light will shine forth therefrom. Master Dogen looked at each individual in such way.

***

Master Dogen taught that we beings who are living life, all the many beings and not just human beings, have such nobility beyond what can be spoken. But that fact is hidden because of the many attachments, desires and other blindnesses whereby we are limited to seeing just a small, ugly little "me." However, just within reach is something great, something just ahead beyond even measure of great or small, which is the self.

... If we polish the self with such purpose, the original light will shine. This is the Buddhist Way; this is our rescue.

215

***

Dogen's words in the Genjo Koan, *"to forget ourself"*, mean to explore through Practice just what is this self – and that Practice is Zazen. By Zazen, this self just naturally ……… [silence]. And to forget in such a way means to enter the world that leaps beyond good and bad. For example, forgetting even that our "self" has the bottomless nobility that I first mentioned, and also forgetting how we fall into the clouds of greed, desire, anger and like folly, one thus leaps beyond both good and bad, which is the meaning of *"to forget ourself."*

***

Dogen's Teacher, Nyojo Zenji, spoke of the sense of small self as *"jinga,"* personhood. The small self is known by a view of "personhood" or "individual selfhood," and with this view something otherwise noble is made small and suffers. When we leave behind and transcend that small selfhood, we find what is real according to Nyojo Zenji.

The words of the Genjo Koan, *"to be experienced by millions of things and phenomena"* then means to leave behind this small self, and to find what I first spoke of, namely that there is a polishing which brings out an interpenetrating, bottomless light of wisdom and benevolence. This is just *Bodhi* (enlightenment, being awakened to the true nature of things), and we find such for ourself right here and thereupon finally let such go. At that moment of letting go there is *"being experienced by millions of things and phenomena."* In other words, in so forgetting the self, we and the universe become one. The Universe is Reality, and Reality and our self become one. And so, there is not separation of self and other, this and that. There is you, there is me. Self is and other is. Yet this is no separation between self and other, and to attain such a pure and expansive heart is *"to be experienced by millions of things and phenomena."*

***

In Shakyamuni's Teachings there is found the words *"Turning the self, Turning the Dharma."* *"Turning the self"* means that one's little self turns the Dharma, and that when one's sense of self is strong, the Dharma is weak. On the other hand, when the Dharma turns the self, then the Dharma is strong and the little self is weak. By this strength, heaven and earth become full of one or the other. By this weakness, there is not left room for even one hair. So, when the little self turns the Dharma, the self is strong and the Dharma is weak. Heaven and earth become full of small self views such that, in that instant, the world is flooded with [greed, anger, ignorance and such] evil, and even a hair's worth of good cannot remain. But when the Dharma turns the self, and the Dharma is strong while the self is weak, then the world of *"being experienced by millions of things and phenomena"* is truly a pure and wonderful world that becomes true for anyone, and manifests the Way. That is how I understand. …

216

Through the generations from Shakyamuni Buddha to Master Bodhidharma and onward, the Ancestors have spoken of *"the Samadhi of One Practice."* Through Zazen, we balance and settle the body while facing the wall, our form of sitting. When we have taken the posture of Zazen, the Dharma turns the self. Zazen is just such Practice. In actuality, with this body, when with the whole body one sits Zazen, the world instantaneously is Dharma and the self turns, and the world becomes a Great Purity whereby no difficulties remain. Because body and mind are one, when the body is made straight and true, the heart responds accordingly and becomes the straightness of Great Purity. Thus, when one person sits one minute of Zazen, the whole world changes to Great Purity.

***

People in the world cannot Practice unless they have a Karmic affinity to do so. Those who cannot Practice are lost in confusion and suffering. It is then a question of what such people should do. There is cause and effect, the cause and the result, such that in making evil and doing bad things one will fall, but making and doing good one will rise. This is the truth of the universe. Each individual's acts of good and bad certainly bear fruit. But because we keep moving forward [in life], when we invite such lost people together to sit Zazen, we can get them heading instead in a good direction. Doing this is the religious heart. This is what I feel is the heart we should carry.

***

We encounter a world of Great Purity free of dust and impurities, and we can encounter all the 10,000 things [all the phenomena of the universe] in this way. … It is a world free of measure and judgments. … For example, if we sit Zazen for one minute, thus there is one minute of Buddha, which is Satori. Satori leads to Satori leads to Satori. It is not just a one time Satori, but the entirety is Satori. What we call "Satori" is the realization spoken of in Master Dogen's teaching *"Practice and Realization are One."* It is much like saying that if we take a single bowl of rice, that one bowl of rice alone can fill our stomach and is everything. This is the Satori of rice. … When we offer Gassho, that is making a Buddha with Gassho, the Satori of Gassho. When we prostrate we make a Buddha, the bow is all, all becomes one. … This is realization, for Satori is not some special sudden moment when light pours forth brightly, something one seeks and acquires suddenly after years of sitting. Not at all. …

***

In Master Dogen's Gakudo Yojinshu, he states, *"In the buddha way, one should always enter and experience enlightenment through Practice. … one should know that arousing Practice in the midst of delusion, one attains enlightenment even before recognizing so."* This *"Practice in the midst of delusion"* means while right amid confusion. As Practice advances, this confusion is the place for a Bodhisattva's merciful and compassionate heart, the kind heart of Buddha, the loving heart of a mother in caring for a child. This is confusion and to be bathed in confusion. A mother may feel that she must do this thing for her beautiful child, or that to help her child, but we might say that each others' mutual bodies are also in a kind of separation and confusion. This skin, flesh, bones and marrow, the whole body, may be called by the name of confusion.
But that confusion, when one is sitting Zazen with the entire body, is Practice amid confusion. Then, this *"attains realization before even recognizing so"* is as Master Dogen said in another writing, Gyobutsu Yuigi, *"Keep in mind that Buddhas, being within the Buddha's Way, do not wait for enlightenment."* Because the many Buddhas do not wait for enlightenment, enlightenment is not something in need of waiting for. Already, right now, each intimate act from morning until night whether walking, standing, sitting or reclining, doing just this to help all the people of this world, wishing to do that other thing, just each individual act is already Satori. One is already in Satori even before experiencing Satori. … Continuing action by action, there is no gap, no missing space.

***

Calligraphy signed "Eihei Rempo"
To See Right Through

To give rise to good mind, to arouse beginner's mind, thereupon to arouse resolve, and then to really take action, are all coming about by Practice. The Buddha Way is actually realized by our making effort, putting all to work with this human body, whereby the Buddha Way first comes to be truly lived.

[Even though we are Originally Enlightened], without actual conduct and cultivation such does not manifest. But to the extent we actually practice this with the limbs and whole body, the skin, flesh, bones and marrow actually embody this and such becomes ours. Otherwise, it is not truly ours and we cannot truly live it. Thus we must Practice.

***

Practice and Realization are One. During the fifty-four years of Master Dogen's life, in writing, washing his face morning and night, all the various actions, sitting, standing, walking, and reclining, drinking tea and eating meals, every such action one-by-one without exception was Practice-Realization. To Practice is Enlightenment, this was Dogen's signature Teaching. He dedicated himself so all through his life as a gift to us. It is just like the compassion felt toward a small grandchild by the loving heart of grandmotherly mind. Master Koun Ejo, the successor to Master Dogen who assisted his Teacher for some twenty years, after his death built a small hut next to his master's grave and continued for some fifty years until his own death … with a sincere and earnest heart, a gentle, loyal mind … to honor and serve his master without once stepping away. However, another student, Master Tettsû Gikai, would supplicate Dogen during his life like a cajoling child pleading to receive Transmission of the Dharma, asking to please be given that noble essence. However, despite this request, because there was yet a lack of a loving, grandmotherly mind in Gikai, in the end he did not receive Dogen's permission before Dogen died [and had to wait for many years]. Truly, when we engage in Practice, unless we lose our small self, we will not be vessels of the truth.

***

Zazen and all our daily actions [study, working, eating and cleaning] naturally come together as whole. If we make sincere effort, it will necessarily be experienced by anyone. What one sows in Practice is what one reaps. This is Karma. The good and bad Karmic actions we do are also what we necessarily come to receive. There is a saying, *"What I sow, another does not reap; what another sows, I do not reap. But what I sow, I reap."* Truly, the way this works is very precise, and it is not difficult to grasp.

Each individual, if in each moment he regulates his walking, standing, sitting or reclining, can open the world of the Dharma.

***

To *"arouse Bodhi mind"* is something that manifests naturally in ourselves. Master Dogen rearranged a bit the words *"arousing Bodhi mind"* so that it became *"Bodhi mind arises."* For a long time, if you just do one thing wholeheartedly and effusively, such will necessarily come pouring out. It is mutual and it is natural. When a child we have put to bed sleeps enough, by himself his eyes will naturally open and he will awake all smiles. But if we suddenly wake him up for some reason, he will cry and complain. So, Master Dogen said "arousing Bodhi mind" becomes "Bodhi mind arises." Master Dogen said in Shobogenzo Zazenshin, *"the first zazen is the first sitting Buddha."* Even if the legs hurt or the body hurts, the first time we sit Zazen, the very first time we sit, is also the very first making of a sitting Buddha. This is what is taught in Shobogenzo Zazenshin. It shows how much our arousing Bodhi mind is noble. If we have the will and put it into Practice, we undertake actual practice and implementation. In other words, if we so engage in Practice-Enlightenment, we naturally make such our own. We must keep endeavoring for the long haul. In our Buddhist words, *"Life after life and world after world, we are born again, we die again."* What is thus transmitted forever is, as Master Dogen states in Genjo Koan, *"Then we can forget the mental trace of realization, and show the real signs of forgotten realization continually, moment by moment."* To keep going so for the very very long term is to have such a heart.

***

What is this forgetting *"traces of enlightenment"* that Master Dogen speaks of?

Everyone seems to be aiming for this thing called "Satori," wondering what kind of incredible, fantastic happening it is, everyone appears to be running after what they consider this rare and wonderful thing. But Satori is just the enlightenment of Practice-Enlightenment, an enlightenment whereby, if one eats just a single bowl of rice, then the belly fills up with one bowl's worth, and then that circulates and fills up one's whole body. To go further and forget even that fact is "forgetting traces of enlightenment." If we receive one bowl, we just smile and that is enough. That is "traces of enlightenment." Then we forget and no thing remains even to name. If we sit for one minute, such is one minute of Buddha, and there is just nothing more. … So, "Then we can forget the mental trace of realization, and show the real signs of forgotten realization continually, moment by moment."

***

I left home to be Ordained at the age of 12 years old. … In those days, Kishizawa Ian Roshi delivered some lectures on the Shobogenzo, and so came for a Shobogenzo Study Group to Shizuoka Prefecture. At that time, my senior brother trainee priest said, because it happened to be just the very next day right after my Ordination, *"Rempo, please come bring some tea and sweets to Roshi's place."* When I asked him, *"How should I offer sweets to the Roshi, what should I say?"* my brother monk said, *"Please do take one."* At that point I don't remember if I kneeled down or bent down or stood up while serving, but I remember saying to the Roshi, *"Please do take one."* And I put out a Japanese sweet beancurd pastry. Smiling and looking at my face, the Roshi said, *"Eh, you will only give me one?"* He laughed. I was really surprised, so I sprang up and ran away. After that, the Roshi was very kind to me for the next fifty years, but after he died what I still remember is, *"Eh, you will only give me one?"* You see, *"One thing is all phenomena,"* all is one. This means that one is all. This is a noble teaching in fact, and for us our every action, each move of the hand or move of the foot, is truly the noble path of the Buddha way. It is taught that our entire self is there.

***

When it is said *"Body-Mind are One,"* this means that the human body in its entirety is the mind. And the mind in its entirety is the human body as well. This is the very fundamental point of the Teachings of Shakyamuni Buddha. We sum it up with the single phrase *"Body-Mind are One,"* and do not divide them into two things. It is a non-Buddhist teaching to divide them into

221

two. It becomes a different teaching. Thus, when the body is straight and true, the mind becomes straight and true. The doorway to the teachings is founded on this "*Body-Mind are One,*" a teaching continuing right to us for 2500 years until today. Body is mind. It is something quite deeper than the ordinary view of world and society.

Niwa Zenji Zazen at Eiheiji Betsuin

APPENDIX II

OBITUARY:

Eight Ways GUDO WAFU NISHIJIMA Will Help Change ZEN BUDDHISM

My Teacher, GUDO WAFU NISHIJIMA ROSHI, passed away on January 28th, 2014, age 94. In manner, he was a soft spoken, gentle, conservative man of his times, born nearly a century ago in Taisho era Japan. In action, he was a perceptive visionary of the future of Buddhism, a great critic of the state of Zen in modern Japan and an outspoken Buddhist reformer (even if largely ignored by the Zen establishment). His students are not all cut of the same cloth, not by any means. Yet I believe his legacy will carry on through many of us in the following eight ways and more.

I will not assert that all are original ideas to Nishijima alone. There are many other people these days who share such views to varying degrees. Nonetheless, what was unique about Nishijima Roshi was how thoroughly and energetically he called for a new vision of Zen Buddhism. Suchness transcends time, place and change, while Buddhist Truth is not dependent on outer wrappings. Yet, Buddhist traditions and practices must constantly change as they encounter new times, places and cultures. I believe that these eight changes, which Nishijima symbolizes, will have lasting effects on the future of Zen in the West; and Treeleaf Sangha, where I am one teacher, is dedicated and committed to their furtherance.

1 – STEPPING THROUGH THE TRADITIONAL FOURFOLD CATEGORIES OF PRIEST & LAY, MALE & FEMALE:
Unlike most Buddhist clergy in Asia, Japanese priests typically marry and are not celibate. Some look at this as a great failing of Japanese Buddhism, a break from twenty-five centuries of tradition. In Japan and the West, even some Japanese lineage priests and lay teachers themselves are unsure of their own identity and legitimacy, and of their roles compared to each other. With great wisdom, Nishijima transcended all such questions and limiting categories. He advocated a way of stepping right through and beyond the whole matter, of finding living expressions where others saw restriction, and of preserving the tradition even as things change. While he was a champion of the celibate way (Nishijima Roshi, although married, turned to a celibate lifestyle for himself upon ordination), he never felt that celibacy was the only road for all priests. Nishijima advocated a form of ordination that fully steps beyond and drops away divisions of "Priest or Lay, Male or Female," yet allows us to fully embody and actuate each and all as the situation requires. In our lineage, we are not ashamed of nor try to hide our sexuality and worldly relationships, nor do we feel conflicted that we are "monks" with kids and mortgages. When I am a parent to my children, I am 100% that and fully there for them. When I am a worker

225

at my job, I am that and embody such a role with sincerity and dedication. And when I am asked to step into the role of hosting Zazen, offering a dharma talk, practicing and embodying our history and teachings and passing them on to others, I fully carry out and embody 100% the role of "Priest" in that moment. Whatever the moment requires: maintaining a Sangha community, bestowing the Precepts, working with others to help sentient beings. The names we call ourselves do not matter. In Nishijima's way, we do not ask and are unconcerned with whether we are "Priest" or "Lay", for we are neither that alone, while always thoroughly both; exclusively each in purest and unadulterated form, yet wholly all at once. It is just as, in the West, we have come to step beyond the hard divisions and discriminations between "male" and "female," recognizing that each of us may embody all manner of qualities to varying degrees as the circumstances present, and that traditional "male" and "female" stereotypes are not so clear-cut as once held. So it is with the divisions of "Priest" and "Lay."

2 – FINDING OUR PLACE OF PRACTICE AND TRAINING "OUT IN THE WORLD":

For thousands of years, it was nearly impossible to engage in dedicated Zen practice except in a monastic setting, to access fellow practitioners, teachers and teachings, to have the time and resources and economic means to pursue serious practice, except by abandoning one's worldly life. By economic and practical necessity, a division of "Priest" and "Lay" was maintained because someone had to grow the food to place in the monks' bowls, earn the wealth to build great temples, have children to keep the world going into the next generation. Although Mahayana figures like Vimalakirti stood for the principle that liberation is available to all, the practical situation was that only a householder with Vimalakirti's wealth, leisure and resources might have a real chance to do so. Now, in modern societies with better distributions of wealth (when compared to the past, because we still have a long way to go), increased 'leisure' time, literacy and education, media access and simpler means of travel and communication across distances, many of the economic and practical barriers to practice and training have been removed. This is the age when we may begin to figuratively "knock down monastery walls," to find that Buddha's Truths may be practiced any place, without divisions of "inside" walls or "outside." For some of us, the family kitchen, children's nursery, office or factory where we work diligently and hard, the hospital bed, volunteer activity or town hall are all our "monastery" and place of training. We can come to recognize the "monastery" located in buildings made of wood and tile as in some ways an expedient means, although with their own power and beauty too. There are still times when each of us can benefit from periods of withdrawal and silence, be it a sesshin or ango, or the proverbial grass hut in distant hills. Yes, this Way still welcomes all manner of people, each pursuing the paths of practice suited to their needs and circumstances, be they temple priests catering to the needs of their parishioners, hermits isolated in caves, celibate monks in mountain monasteries, or "out in the world" types demonstrating that all can be found right in the city streets and busy highways of this modern world. Nishijima, a Zen priest yet a working man, a husband and father most of his life, stood for a dropping of "inside" and "out." He was someone who knew the value of times of retreat, but also the constant realization of these teachings in the home, workplace and soup kitchens.

3 – SAVING ZEN PRACTICE FROM THE 'FUNERAL CULTURE' DOMINANT IN JAPAN & THE CREEPING INSTITUTIONALIZATION APPEARING IN THE WEST: Buddhist priests in Japan play an important role in soothing the hearts of their parishioners during times of mourning. Funerals and memorial services are important aspects of Japanese tradition, as in all cultures. However, Japanese Zen, and other flavors of Buddhism, have become excessively focused on "funeral culture" almost to the exclusion of all else. Except for shining lights scattered here and there who try to keep the ways of Dogen and Zazen alive, most Japanese Soto Zen priests do not even bother with the sitting of Zazen after their youthful training stint in the monastery. The massive Buddhist institutions of Japan, including the Rinzai and Soto schools, have become licensing guilds turning out conveyor belt priests (usually temple sons compelled into training in order to take over the "funeral business" franchise of their family's managed temple). Nishijima was ordained and received Dharma Transmission from Rempo Niwa Zenji, subsequently the Abbot of Eihei-ji, the senior Soto Zen monastery. Knowing that Nishijima was a critic of the whole system he would come to head as the eventual leader of the Soto Sect, Niwa nonetheless empowered Nishijima as a teacher based on Niwa's own shared desire to help reform Soto Zen. Right now, in America and Europe, there is a tendency among some big Zen institutions themselves to grow into large Zen "churches", institutions concerned with preserving their own views of doctrinal "Orthodoxy", with preserving their status, the authority of their priests, their rights to determine the legitimacy of Ordinations, all by themselves establishing domestic systems of guild membership. Of course, the maintenance of basic standards for priest training and ethics are very necessary and to be applauded. Our Treeleaf Sangha fully supports such efforts. The question, however, is where to draw the line between needed standards and helpful training, versus certain groups' protecting their own primacy, exclusivity, authority and narrow dogma.

4 – OFFERING A HOME TO ZEN FOLKS WHO ARE REFUGEES FROM INSTITUTIONALISM, SECT POLITICS AND SCANDAL IN CERTAIN PARTS OF THE ZEN WORLD: Nishijima provided a haven for many vibrant Zen teachers who were excluded or isolated within other Zen groups in Europe, America and Japan. The situations took many forms: people fleeing the internal politics and factionalism in the Sangha where they first practiced; those blocked by glass ceilings and closed guilds in Japan and elsewhere; Japanese uninterested in joining "funeral culture"; those fleeing cultish behavior and unethical teachers; Christian clergy interested in practicing Zen as Christians; gifted Zen priests and teachers interested in combining Zen practice with home, work and "in the world" life without desire or ambition for monastic training; and people alienated by the doctrinal interpretations and dogma they were encountering in other groups. I often refer to this bunch, very diverse in character and personality, as the "Island of Misfit Zen Toys" (referring to an old children's program in the US seen each year at Christmas, about an island where all the broken and misfit toys went to live from Santa's workshop until they found a home). Nishijima provided a home to such folks, each very devoted to this Zen path in his or her own sincere way. Our Treeleaf Sangha, and Nishijima's other students, will continue to serve as a haven for other "misfit toys" in the future.

5 – A RESPECT FOR TRADITION, YET AN EMPHASIS ON FINDING NEW EXPRESSIONS SUITABLE FOR MODERN TIMES AND WESTERN CULTURE:

Nishijima was thoroughly imbued with the spirit of Dogen, was (with his student Chodo Cross) the translator of Dogen's complete Shobogenzo into modern Japanese and English, and held that Master Dogen had found ways to express the Buddhist teachings rarely heard until that time. Nonetheless, despite his profound trust in the teachings of Dogen, Nishijima was never a prisoner of Dogen. Among the many treasured teachings of Dogen, which are timeless and survive the centuries, Nishijima knew that others were primarily the views and expressions of a man living amid the society and superstitions of 12th century Japan. Those of Dogen's writings directed primarily to his band of monks at Eiheiji and elsewhere must be placed side-by-side with Dogen's other pronouncements recognizing the possibilities of Zen practice for people in all situations in life. The teachings of Dogen are not simply for monks isolated in the snowy mountains, but are for all of us. His words, if appropriate only to his day and culture, should be left to his day and culture. Buddhism, and Dogen's teachings, can be brought forth and adapted for our places and times. Is this not so for the teachings of so many of our Zen ancestors beyond Dogen too? I remember, for example, asking Nishijima once about the "right way" to conduct a "Soto Zen funeral" for a good friend who had died in America. Nishijima told me that ultimately I should make a new, heartfelt ritual to honor my friend. He told his students in America, Europe and elsewhere to do things in sincere ways suitable for our cultures and societies, inspired by tradition perhaps, yet finding new ways to express the same.

6 – AN INTERPRETATION OF ZAZEN AS THE FULFILMENT OF REALITY ITSELF:

One key aspect of Dogen's teachings that Nishijima fully danced, and all his students dance with him, is that Zazen is the fulfillment of Reality itself. On that, nothing more is in need of saying here.

7 – LOOKING FOR COMMON GROUND AND THE COMPATIBILITY OF BUDDHIST TEACHINGS, ZEN AND ZAZEN WITH WESTERN PHILOSOPHY AND SCIENCE:

Like D.T. Suzuki, Masao Abe and other Japanese Zen figures of his time, Nishijima thought that Zen teachings could best be introduced to a Western audience by finding common ground with Western philosophy. Years before it was common to load meditators into MRI machines, Nishijima spoke of the connection of Zazen to the brain and human nervous system, influenced by the then cutting-edge research on meditation and the so-called "relaxation response" by Harvard's Dr. Herbert Benson and others. However, I wish to say honestly that Nishijima was not a professional philosopher nor a trained scientist. He tried to express from his own heart all encountered in Zazen. For that reason, he frequently spoke in very personal and, perhaps, too simplified ways on both Western philosophical concepts and, as a scientific layman, about all that is happening in the body and brain. It is only in recent years that we have come to understand that many separate physiological and neurological systems are interlinked in complex ways, each coming to play in Zazen and meditation. Nevertheless, Nishijima stood for the meeting and fundamental compatibility of Buddhist tenets and scientific method.

8 – AVOIDING SUPERSTITION, FANTASY, MIRACLES & MAGICAL INCANTATION IN BUDDHISM: One person's "sacred and cherished belief" is another person's "fantasy and nonsense." Sometimes seemingly exotic practices and legends can possess a psychological power and poetry that opens the human heart, even if not "literally true." While recognizing that fact, Nishijima Roshi sought to present Zen practice freed of naive beliefs and superstitions, exaggerated claims and idealized myths masquerading as historical events even in our own Zen traditions, all of which can bury and hide the very real power of our Buddhist way in a fog of ignorance and foolishness. I, and many of his other students, join him in that task.

In such eight ways, and many others, Gudo Wafu Nishijima changed Zen Buddhism and continues to do so. His legacy lives on in his many students around the world and his teachings will further enrich and transform our tradition into the future.

Jundo Cohen, Treeleaf Sangha

GUDO WAFU NISHIJIMA ROSHI PASSED AWAY ON JANUARY 28th, 2014
HIS MANY STUDENTS AROUND THE WORLD RECALL OUR TEACHER

19424784R00139

Made in the USA
San Bernardino, CA
25 February 2015